10 Leadership Styles for Highly Effective Project Managers

10 LEADERSHIP STYLES FOR HIGHLY EFFECTIVE PROJECT MANAGERS

A Personal, Professional, and Empirical Look Into Best Practice Leadership Styles for Every Project Manager

Michael Dale, Ph.D.

Copyright © 2023 by Michael Dale, Ph.D.

All rights reserved. No part of this book may be reproduced or used in any manner without written permission of the copyright owner except for the use of quotations in a book review.

DEDICATION

In this unique moment, I wish to express my heartfelt love and admiration for my wife, Trina, whose unwavering support over our 26 years together has been the cornerstone of my personal and professional achievements. To my three cherished children, Maniyah, Brianna, and Michael II, I owe you much of who I have become and aspire to be.

A special gratitude extends to my dear parents, who have molded and shaped my thinking and instilled in me the values of empathy, civility, and the pursuit of success. Thank you so much.

Jude 24-25 NLT:

[24] Now all glory to God, who is able to keep you from falling away and will bring you with great joy into his glorious presence without a single fault. [25] All glory to him who alone is God, our Savior through Jesus Christ our Lord. All glory, majesty, power, and authority are his before all time, and in the present, and beyond all time! Amen.

TABLE OF CONTENTS

PART I: A PERSONAL JOURNEY INTO LEADERSHIP

Prologue 10
- *A 30-year Journey* 12
- *The Beginning of Something Special* 13
- *A Big Opportunity* 16
- *A Special Place* 17
- *Looking Back* 19
- *Back to the Beginning* 23
- *Starting to Grow* 27
- *On the Right Path* 29
- *First Job Lessons Learned* 32

PART II: WHY 10 LEADERSHIP STYLES?

Chapter 1: Project Professional Leadership Style 47

Chapter 2: Skills-based Leadership Style 53

Chapter 3: Style Leadership Approach......................... 56

Chapter 4: Situational Leadership Style 63

Chapter 5: Path-Goal Leadership Style 67

Chapter 6: Contingency Leadership Style..................... 71

Chapter 7: Emotional Intelligence Leadership Style 73
- *Trait Model of Emotional Intelligence.* 75

- *Ability Model of Emotional Intelligence.* 76
- *Mixed Model of Emotional Intelligence.* 76

Chapter 8: Christian Leadership Style 79
- *Godly Leadership* 82
- *Good Judgment* 83

Chapter 9: Servant Leadership Style 86
- *Principles of servant leadership* 91
- *Servant leaders are emotionally intelligent* 92
- *Servant leadership in business* 93
- *Servant leadership in the Bible* 95
- *Project Manager and Servanthood* 100

Chapter 10: Transformational Leadership Style 106

PART III: AN EMPIRICAL STUDY OF LEADERSHIP

Chapter 11: An Inductive Look into Leadership 113
- *Discussion of the Study.* 115
- *Implications of the Study* 118
- *Leadership Training* 118
- *Dominate Leadership Styles* 119
- *Best Results Leadership Style* 121
- *Effective Project Managers* 122

Chapter 12: Final Thoughts and Conclusions 125

References 131

Appendix - Dale Leadership Effectiveness Matrix 140

PART I

A PERSONAL JOURNEY INTO LEADERSHIP

PROLOGUE

Between a bachelor's degree, an MBA, and a PhD, it would seem that I have written 12 books already! During the development of my thesis and dissertation, there were several 30-page papers about management, business, and leadership. I feel like I have the background and knowledge to write comprehensively on either subject. However, a 20-year career in project management has led me down this path to author the *10 Leadership Styles for Highly Effective Project Managers*.

My thoughtful deliberation included some questions about what would be most appealing to potential readers who I thought *may* read this book: What would they *want* to purchase and read about? Is project management well covered from all available directions? Will my thoughts be drowned out by 100s of authors who came before me and

PROLOGUE

sojourned on the subject? Indeed, the subject of project management has amassed a considerable body of research and literature.

Outside the inner world of project management practitioners, the typical reader would be hard-pressed to name a single author who has written about the subject. Project management writers have spoken overwhelmingly to experienced practitioners, except for a few popular books about the basics. The *10 Leadership Styles for Highly Effective Project Managers* does not endeavor to be a first but an addition. It was in the second year of my PhD program at Carolina University that I first encountered advice from a faculty member who said, "The best dissertations add to well-founded prepositions rather than create new ones." I was impressed enough to begin a thorough search of founded dissertation topics that deserved another look, which made my experience and journey richer. My dissertation successfully traversed 2 important subject matters and provided empirical evidence of the relationship between *leadership* and *successful projects*. Here is where we begin to look into my personal leadership journey.

PROLOGUE

A 30-YEAR JOURNEY

My life of leadership started 30 years ago as a high school student at the now-demolished Ensley High School in Birmingham, Alabama. I was not keenly interested in the subject of leadership yet at that time. I eventually attended two or three meetings of the FBLA (Future Business Leaders of America) in 10th and 11th grade. However, I never quite "joined" FBLA. I mostly sat and listened to the established professionals invited by the organization to speak and encourage undecided kids like me. I was interested in business leadership but was not aware or knowledgeable about what I would like to do for a career.

My first "stint" with leadership would be in the form of a position in JROTC (Junior Reserve Officer Training Core). As a freshman, I took my first class in JROTC, assuming the rank of a private first class. Through hard work, commitment, and a pair of shiny boots, I would ascend to the rank of Captain by my junior year. With this rank, I was selected by JROTC instructors to become a Company Commander, leading over 75 fellow students. This position required some leadership characteristics but mostly the ability to start the class day with a hardy, "Company, Attention!" Then,

PROLOGUE

depending on what was being announced, or maybe some news to be shared, I would follow that command up with "at ease!" This showed my confidence, competence, and authority using just two words. At the early age of 16, this was the most that was expected. **At this point, I learned that a seat of authority carried immense influence and held the capability to affect others dramatically just through the issuance of a single command.** There were two other company commanders who reigned over their classes, but by far, I had the largest and most impressive group of students under my guard. For the school year, this would lend me a level of respect and prestige from the students, at least from those who were part of JROTC.

THE BEGINNING OF SOMETHING SPECIAL

In my senior year of high school, I had my second experience of leading others. I tried out for the football team in the spring of my freshman year and worked hard over the next couple of years to become a decent player. Much of my sophomore and junior years had been filled with co-star opportunities, never chances to really shine. Towards the end of my junior year, I began to fill out and grow more physical statues. I found that muscle building came naturally

PROLOGUE

to me, unlike some of the other scrawny kids around me. Either that, or they refused to work hard in the weight room to build more muscle. I found myself spending hours in the weight room trying to achieve the ultimate physique. Then, another friend introduced me to John Weider's amino acids, which allowed me to lift heavier weights for a longer time. Using the John Weider program, I was able to enter my senior year at an ideal size and speed for playing my position. In my senior year, I was very successful on the football field, earning the title of Captain of the football team.

As Captain of the football team, I did not provide traditional leadership to the team. This means that I did not direct the activities, set the agenda, or provide any inspiration to my teammates. There were others on the team without the title of Captain who performed in these capacities. **In hindsight, I would come to understand why focusing on strengths is a better use of a leader's time while delegating the performance of weak areas to more capable team members.** The coaches selected me as Captain because of various other factors that were unknown to me at the time. At this early phase in my leadership career, the coaches did not rely on me for verbal things. I was very loyal and committed to the job. So, I was trustworthy to complete the assignments that I was given to the best of my ability, which provided an ideal example of what the coaches were looking for in each player. I was also helpful and considerate of the people around me, not having much of an egotistical attitude associated with your typical football star player. I treated people with respect on and off the field, which garnered recognition and admiration from people in authority.

My teammates weren't as receptive to my methods. In high school, the objective is to be cool and fit in where you can so that assimilation can occur. There are cliques, groups, and associations that typically help a high school student to find his or her place on the social ladder. On the football team, it was no different. The only exception was that a high school football team is a clique in and of itself. So, smaller groups within the clique are even more exclusively created, primarily revolving around position or role on the team. For a reason unknown to me then, I disassociated myself from the crowd, daring to be alone. Often, I felt more comfortable escaping the assimilation and decided to create my own way of approaching the landscape.

PROLOGUE

A BIG OPPORTUNITY

In college, I was humbled to have been awarded a full scholarship to play football. I was not heavily recruited by many colleges. I would say 11 showed some interest. Their interest was mostly displayed by constant visits to my high school and home phone calls. Some college coaches would quietly visit the football office, make inquiries about my abilities, and watch highlight films. Others would obtain films of my best games and formulate a sincere curiosity in me. Samford University, one of the 11 schools, was not interested in me at first. Samford visited my high school to look at another teammate to whom they intended to offer a full scholarship. From what I was told, the Samford coach inquired, "Who is that coming off the end so fast?" From then on, Samford wanted to know more about me, and interest grew from there. **It is true that existing talent is far less critical than the potential for greatness.**

I was invited for an official visit to Samford in the Spring of my senior year. The official visit entailed an overnight stay in a hotel close to Samford. Still, much of the two-day visit would be spent touring the university's football facilities and meeting the coaches. I am not 100% sure, but

PROLOGUE

I do not think head Coach Terry Bowden was completely sold on making me an official offer until we met. On the last day of the visit, my mom, dad, and I were invited to an exclusive meeting with Coach Bowden. The meeting started with Coach Bowden expressing a list of niceties about my family and upbringing. It seemed like there was a slow but meaningful build-up to his climatic statement, "We'd like to have you as a part of the team." I did not fully expect the offer on the spot, so I did not express any acceptance then and there. I did have at least three or four other offers that I was contemplating as well. But by far, this was the offer that I was the proudest of on the list.

A SPECIAL PLACE

For me, Samford was a very special place that I had come to know a year earlier while participating in a program called Boys State. Boys State was a selective program where two boys from about 100 high schools were invited to Samford to participate in mock government exercises for three days. It was three of the best days of my life because coming from sort of a conservative African American background and environment rendered me somewhat sheltered. Seeing 200 boys from all walks of life, colors, creeds, and ethnicities broadened my thought patterns. The experience was life-changing, and the facilities at Samford were the best I had ever seen of all the colleges I would visit going forward. I often teased people about Samford by saying, "You could eat off the ground; that's how clean and manicured everything was." I did not know until my official visit that the school building architecture was called "Georgian Colonial", which carries a rich history of monumental beauty across Samford's sprawling edifices.

So, on the official NCAA signing day in February 1992, I signed a scholarship acceptance letter in the library of Ensley High School. My high school coaches accompanied me: Curtis Coleman, Mitzi Jackson, and Sylvester Campbell. My mom, dad, and some teachers were present as well. There was even a cadre of television news outlets who attended to take pictures and record the event. I was extremely proud of my accomplishment of achieving what seemed to be an impossible idea just three years earlier. On that day, I realized that I was destined to be more than some gave me credit for, but exactly what some had recognized in me from an early age.

PROLOGUE

LOOKING BACK

Each experience that I had up until signing day was meaningful and contributed to the culmination of the event. As my coaches proudly congratulated me, I was mindful of their lessons and contributions to who I had become and what I would become. Coach Jackson, a really "cool" coach who seemed to be as young as the players, had endless energy. He would race wide receivers, run crisp routes, and throw picture-perfect passes. He was our offensive coordinator. He was laid back and assertive when needed but very confident in who he was. I do not recall which college Coach Jackson played for, but he was a star running back. He was good enough to have made it to the NFL and played for the Kansas City Chiefs (I could be wrong about the team). But just from the knowledge of him having played in the League, he garnered a lot of respect from the players. Ultimately, whether we were good or bad players, we all played the game with aspirations of going to college and, if extremely fortunate, going further.

Coach Jackson was the only "professional athlete" role model that I had in my life at this time. The person that I imagined I would imitate my professional football career

PROLOGUE

after. At that point, he was the closest reference point that I had to a successful athlete. He lived up to the elite professional role that we all knew he was capable of one day when practice got a little out of hand. We had one kid on the team who was a pariah of trouble. I will not mention names, but readers who were on the team at the time will know this story. Anyways, this kid was a wide-receiver and would constantly run routes that Coach Jackson was not happy with. On this day, this kid ran a route, and Coach Jackson expressed his discontent with the outcome. This kid decided to yell back at Coach in a tone that was not very respectful to authority, and Coach did not like it. None of this was recorded on videotape (I wish it were), but I recall this kid getting into Coach Jackson's face, and a physical scuffle ensued. It was not a fistfight, but Coach Jackson made sure that this kid understood in no uncertain terms that verbal or physical aggression would be tolerated. Coach subdued this kid firmly and held him down until he cowed. I do not recall any players testing Coach Jackson after that!

  Coach Sylvester Campbell was our defensive coordinator. I think Coach Campbell was the first to notice that I had an inkling of potential talent. I may have been 5'8 and 170 lbs. that spring in 1989 when I first tried out for the football

PROLOGUE

team. I did not know anything about football, really. Having grown up in the Northern part of the US, the game of choice was baseball. But I was more interested in football because it was the most popular sport in the South. In the first couple of days of tryouts, I worked out with the quarterbacks and wide receivers. Because of my size and lankiness, I thought either position would fit. However, the offense was an option set in an "I-formation," which meant that the quarterback needed good footwork. For some reason, I could never quite get the option offense down-packed, so I was noticeably looking out of place.

One day, Coach Campbell noticed my discomfort and said he thought I could be a better fit on defense. From then on, Coach took me under his wing and spent a lot of time teaching me the fundamentals of defensive positions, techniques, stances, etc. He would pull me aside a lot to explain what was going on and quiz me on how I would handle a real game situation. He always said that I had a lot of physical potential. Coach was the first to mention the name "Biscuit" to me. He said, "You remind me of Biscuit and the way he played when he was here at Ensley." Biscuit was Cornelius Bennet. He was a standout linebacker/defensive end who graduated from Ensley High School

PROLOGUE

in 1983. Bennet signed a full scholarship offer to play at University of Alabama and earned All-American honors there, achieving celebrity status. Bennet went on to play 13 years in the NFL, achieving Pro-Bowl status multiple times in his sensational career. Being compared to Biscuit was a high praise! One that I tried my best to live up to and pattern some of my skillset to achieve. Having the encouragement of Coach Campbell helped me to navigate my growth as a player and always aim high toward my greatest potential.

Coach Curtis Coleman was a unique character in my life, starting at the age of 14. We met in 1988 when I was a freshman in high school trying to find myself. My first choice of extracurricular activities was basketball. Much like football, I thought it would be cool to be a basketball player and garner some popularity from it. At that time in my life, I was struggling to be noticed and recognized. I had an unusual desire to be accepted and hoped to be great at something. Basketball came somewhat easy to me. I had some natural ability for jumping and rebounding. It was during this time that I recall asking my father for help. I wanted to become a better shooter, so I asked my dad for some tips.

PROLOGUE

It was a sunny Saturday morning when Dad took my brother David and me to a nearby court to demonstrate the art of shooting a basketball. My dad was a high school standout track star on a state championship team. But he had played some basketball and knew his way around the court. His advice that day would be impactful, perhaps legendary in my mind. I am not sure where or who trained or mentored him in the game of basketball. However, he explained that it was "all in the wrist."... Shooting the ball was all in the flick of the wrist. Dad demonstrated the procedure and made some good shots that day. I decided this was a key to the game, and I have kept it as on-court advice, even with my kids.

BACK TO THE BEGINNING

Back to Coach Curtis Coleman, who was perhaps the most influential person to enter my life as a freshman in high school. I first met him as I lined up with the rest of the boys, trying out for the junior varsity basketball squad. He was a dominant figure, very sure of himself, particularly about how he carried himself. He had a vibrant personality, caring and direct about what he wanted to accomplish. If he saw potential in you, he would try to mold it. Even when

PROLOGUE

potential was bleak, I have seen him encourage, support, and steer kids in the right direction. I was no different than the other 30 kids trying out that day for the JV basketball team. I was skinny, quiet, and a little uncoordinated. Instead of remaining an unnoticed freshman, I caught Coach Coleman's eye, but not in a good way.

It was the third day of tryouts, and I was one of the 30 who had lasted through all the cuts. Every day before, there had been a piece of paper posted on the gym wall with the names of the boys who had made it to the next tryout, and I had made it through the first two cuts. The tryout list was down to 18 boys, and a typical JV team was 11 to 13 players. I had my sights on capturing this mountain of a goal, which, in hindsight, would be the first team I would ever make. Unfortunately, the third tryout went oddly different than the first two. Coach seemed to be in a different mode that day. He focused more on physical discipline, mental toughness, and what I would later learn was a real word, "sticktoitness." This was also the first time I would hear the phrase "fight through adversity", which would ring in my ears in nearly every predicament, challenge, and struggle to come in my life. This day was less about basketball and more about

PROLOGUE

weeding out the kids who were not ready to be a part of a team. And I was not ready.

It was towards the middle of the tryout. We were running layup drills full court. The drill went something like this: The player would run down the court and make a layup, then he'd run to the opposite end where another player was attempting a layup and play defense. I had run up and down the court at least three times and was completely depleted. I was having trouble making a good layup, and my defense on the other end of the court was ineffective. Regardless, Coach was not letting me off easy. He yelled, "Do it again!" which meant I had to run the full length of the court a fourth time with no rest. By then, my effort was half-paced. I had never been pushed physically. After the fourth and final run down the court, where I literally jogged, Coach yelled, "If you can't give full effort, just quit!" And I did. There was an exit door near the middle of the gym halfway down the court. I stumbled to that door, pushed the handle, yelled back to Coach Coleman, "I don't need this!" and walked out the door. It was sunny outside that door, much as opposed to the dark and musky court I had just run exhaustively on. I sat outside the door gasping for air yet enjoying the release of pressure that had been lifted off me. I thought to myself that no one was going

PROLOGUE

to abuse me or embarrass me in front of my peers. I was sure that Coach had it out for me and tried to make an example of a loser. But Alas! I got the last laugh by defanging him from humiliating me any further, or so I believed in my 14-year-old brain devoid of proportionate challenges.

Little did I know that Coach Coleman was also the head football coach. Five months later, I aspired to free myself of my basketball failures by trying out for the football team in April 1989. By then, I was just another kid amongst nearly 50 football players on the field trying out for the team. Fortunately for me, I was able to stay unnoticed as the kid who quit and walked out of the basketball gym. In fact, no one really remembered me at all. I was not a popular kid at that time and did not have many friends. So, there were no reminders or associations to pair me with. I originally tried out for an offensive position, so I avoided Coach Coleman at first, who was primarily a defensive coach who spent time with the linebackers.

I would later find out that Coach Coleman was a star football player who had a phenomenal career at Livingston College in Alabama. He was very proud of his school, his career, and what he had accomplished. He always spoke about "having some sort of pride about yourself." He believed that respect, honor, and success were earned by a man who respected himself enough to put his best forward. He preached this sentiment the entire spring season during football tryouts. Pride is a word that I thought originated with Coach Coleman at that time. Having pride was forever part of my approach to the game, relationships, and life. **Regardless of the circumstance, dilemma or issue I faced, I could see my Coach say, "Have some pride about yourself!"**.

STARTING TO GROW

I would go on to make the football team and become one of Coach Coleman's favorite players (so I believe). I bought into his message and began not to give up when the going got tough or when adversity reared its ugly head. On the football field, I pushed through physical pain, mental mistakes, and emotional rollercoasters. I believed in myself enough to put my very best forward. My commitment and dedication were noticed by Coach Coleman, who made me Captain of the team in my senior year. By this time, I was the starting outside linebacker for Ensley High School and a star player on the team. I was fast, evasive, and strong, which made me a perfect fit for my position. Coach Coleman had become an authoritative figure in my life that I relied on for high moral judgment, confidence, and the determination between what was right and wrong. His words of encouragement and affirmation of who he believed I could become was meaningful. He warned that there would be distractions, such as "those jokers that did not want to go anywhere in life."

Coach would give me a ride home often after practice. So, I would have to wait until after every kid was picked up, all teachers were gone, and the school was locked up. It would be me and Coach straightening up the locker room, organizing the office, and turning off the gym lights. During the silence of the day's end, I would come to know Coach personally. After having taught school all day and coached all evening, he still has the job of husband and father waiting on him at home. Often exhausted, he still had a lesson or two to teach on the way home. I would listen quietly. On one night home, he talked about some of my teammates. He explained how their environments limited their potential and how much harder it was for them to fight their way through a desperate situation constrained by poverty, drugs, or a hostile environment. He said, "Football is the only thing keeping them off the street; without it, they'll end up like their older brothers or fathers." Football was a way out. Two guys in particular played on the team that Coach would talk about often. They were gentle giants with enormous talent, athleticism, and skill. Both were from not-so-good situations at home but had a gentle and humble spirit. Coach would say, "If I could just get them away from those streets", then maybe there would be hope. But he could not. These two naturally gifted and talented kids would ultimately not stay on the team but drift back into the street life that pulled on them heavily. Knowing his desire to impact the lives of young men, Coach Coleman probably spent more time thinking about these failures than his successes. **Most people breathe more life into their failures than into their successes.** I would hope that I was one of his successes, a reflection of his concerted energy and push to fulfill God-given talent and reach a higher calling.

ON THE RIGHT PATH

In the fall of 1992, I was a freshman on the Samford University campus. Since I was on a full athletic scholarship, my football schedule of training, practice, and games took up most of any free time that I had. When not in the weight room or class, I was fulfilling my scholarship duties. At this time, Samford tuition, books, boarding, and fees were a

PROLOGUE

mere 15K a year. Today, a full scholarship is closer to a 50K price tag! My freshman year was normal. I decided to major in International Business, which was not an official major; however, my academic advisor agreed to put some courses together to achieve a similar goal. Basically, I would be a business school major with a minor in a foreign language.

By my senior year at Samford, I had amassed a few considerable experiences that would afford me a beneficial introduction to the real world. I was selected as Captain of the Football team. It seemed like a similar appointment, much like high school, but this time, the stakes were entirely higher. I had survived a couple of major injuries during my sophomore and junior years that cost me a shot at the pros, but I was still a good player. Before all the injuries, I received some awards, including Pre-season All-Star for the conference.

Off the field, I began to discover that there was more that I could aim to achieve besides athletic accolades. In the Fall of 1996, I became one of the six charter members of the first Black fraternity at Samford—Kappa Alpha Psi (KAY). Furthermore, I was elected the first Polemarch (President) of the chapter known as Omicron Alpha (OA). As a 19-year-old, I did not fully recognize the significance of this achievement. I would later discover that other Black fraternities had tried to

PROLOGUE

establish chapters on Samford's campus to no avail. However, because of the fraternity's rich history of high standards and academic achievement, KAY met the distinguished requirements. In addition, former student Leonardus Eason provided sponsorship and leadership to ensure the charter was successful. Much of the chapter's presence on Samford's campus is owed to Mr. Eason.

Before leaving Samford, I committed much of my time to extracurricular roles in leadership. I worked with the Student Government Association as a Diversity Liaison, hosting retreats and special programs that highlight ethnicity and various cultures. In the role of Vice President of the Black Student Association, I was able to join with other Black students and voice the need for belonging and inclusion ideas that were heard and addressed by school faculty and administration. As a result of these roles and leadership positions, I was given the John R Mott Community Leadership Award. This would be the apex of my senior year upon graduating. It is a prestigious honor for a student to receive this accolade, which names the student who has exhibited the highest ideals of community engagement and excellence in leadership.

PROLOGUE

FIRST JOB LESSONS LEARNED

In the late Fall of 1997, I accepted my first professional job straight out of college. While the pay was terrible, I was elated to be gainfully employed as an Assistant Manager and Loan Officer at First Family Financial, a retail lending office. My rank and position afforded me some indirect authority over loan officers and customer service representatives who had been at the office a lot longer than I had. My first task as a leader was to garner support and respect for the title of Assistant Manager. As anyone could imagine, a 22-year-old was not going to blaze into any business office of mature professionals and easily secure allegiance. If anything, I learned how to work on a team and how to be a team player. There is only one goal in any business: to make a profit. But here is what I learned at First Family that has been useful and retainable throughout my career: **A leader must *set clear objectives and expectations* and *create an environment for open and honest feedback*.** Accordingly, each team member should have a written job delineation that includes clear expectations. Without it, how could anyone be held accountable for their duties? How could they be measured for success or failure at any given point?

PROLOGUE

Besides a written job delineation created to set expectations from the company, each team member should have opportunities for open dialogue to provide feedback to one another. In his 2002 best-seller *The Five Dysfunctions of a Team*, Patrick Lencioni says that a team that holds each other accountable *ensures that poor performers feel pressure to improve.* Now, this should not be a daily event. And it must be the right pressure. For example, when I decided to take lessons from a real instructor to learn how to swim, he used "good pressure" to teach me.

When attempting to float, he gently applied some pressure with his hand placed methodically on my back to keep me balanced. I felt a sense of security knowing that my body would not sink to the bottom of the pool because of his faithful hand placement. On the opposite end of the spectrum, there is "bad pressure." I recall, at the age of 10, visiting the neighborhood recreation center where there was a public pool. I could not swim, but neither could the rest of the kids. So, we typically played in the pool rather than swam. One day, while playing in the deep section of the pool, another kid put pressure on my head and held me underwater. I almost drowned! This attempt at teaching me a lesson about playing in the deep part of the pool was unsolicited. I guess the lesson was that I should keep my guard up and always protect myself. Definitely a well-learned lesson, but I would call the pressure of his hand on my head while I gasped for air a bad kind of pressure!

Secondly, Lencioni says that an accountable team *identifies potential problems quickly by questioning one another's approaches without hesitation.* I learned how to curtail and reduce risk from a senior loan officer at First Family. At the office, our core business was providing small signature loans and mortgage refinances. We would open and close the loans right there in the office. A senior loan officer took me under her wing shortly after my first day on the job. Nicki was smart, well-liked and knew the business inside and out. After overhearing my interaction with my first mortgage loan customer, Nicki quickly made corrections that helped me. Nicki asked me, "Why did you not offer the mortgage insurance to the customer?" I did not think it was important because it would have made a high-interest loan higher, and I wanted to do everything I could to lower the rate. But Nicki explained, **"It is not your job to answer questions that the customers should answer".** I needed to communicate the benefits, discuss the need, and give them the option to accept or reject the mortgage insurance. This lesson in my young career helped me realize that customers are not monolithic and certainly not like me. I needed to allow the customer to make decisions that were best for their financial protection and tolerance for debt. Continuously after, Nicki provided ongoing feedback and asked critical questions to make me think about why it was important to do things the right way.

Thirdly, Lencioni deduces that a responsible team *establishes respect among team members who are held to the same high standards.* The best teams I have participated in had great individual members. Were they great individual people? The answer to that question is emphatically "No!" But in a team dynamic, they fit quite well into the culture and fabric of the team. There was a reciprocal measure of respect for the importance of each team member's role, experience, and contribution to the work. In 2013, I returned from a two-day training for the Certified Scrum Master (CSM). At this early juncture, Agile had not yet received its commercial lift. Scrum had not left the runway at all. I may, at that time, have been the only CSM at BBVA Compass Bank, where I worked as an Application Team Lead and Project Manager. Establishing a team that would follow the precepts of Agile seemed nearly impossible, but I was headstrong in putting

PROLOGUE

my best foot forward. I began by establishing a makeshift scrum team from my current development group.

Three of my developers, Vinod, Srini and Sam, seemed amiable to the idea, but I am sure they recognized it was not fully thought out. In fact, I think I referred to it as iterative development instead of Agile to avoid any resistance. My business lead customer, Dan, would be the acting Product Owner (PO) who rounded out the somewhat organized scrum team. Without using too many scrum terms and concepts, I moved the team from a predictive model of executing work to an adaptive approach where several enhancements and updates were delivered in iterations with little documentation, maximum customer interaction and laser focus on the product. If nothing else was concluded from this first take at an Agile approach, I think the level of respect was raised for each team member's crucial spoke in the wheel. The first tenet of the 2001 Agile Manifesto explains the value of individuals and interactions over processes and tools. Why is this important? **High standards cannot be expressed or achieved through the creation of policy, procedures, or rules; they can only be achieved through personal and professional interactions with people.**

Fourthly, Lencioni prescribes that an accountable team *avoids excessive bureaucracy around performance management and corrective action.* An issue that faces plan-driven teams is the bureaucracy of the emergence of phase gates and approvals needed before passing a certain stage in the completion of work. Although the process is useful and required in specific scenarios, it should not be catered into every team dynamic. In today's environment, "working agreements" seem to work better for small, cohesive teams who work on high-value changes in a dedicated timeframe. Teams who practice an Agile approach to managing work can attest to this method of engagement that reduces the amount of process required. In lieu of processes, the team has working agreements that they agree to at the project's outset. For those of you who would dare not replace a process or procedure that has worked so well for your team in the past, here are some of the key differences between working agreements and traditional team processes:

Table 1: Working Agreements vs. Traditional Processes

Questions	Team Working Agreements	Team Process and Procedures
Who creates?	The entire team creates working agreements together. This can happen in an Agile planning meeting or workshop.	Process Owner

Implicit or Explicit agreement?	Since the working agreement includes a physical interaction between team members and results in a physical document(s), there are implicit and explicit conclusions drawn.	Explicit only
Allows social questions to be addressed?	Yes. A discussion regarding the social system and expectations of the team is a very important tenet of working agreements.	Typically, No.
Allows for a measure of team creativity to engage in desired areas?	Yes. The team interaction is an open discussion moderated by the team leader or scrum master if Agile is being used.	Typically, No.
Can it be modified?	Yes. Working agreements are based on the team, not the project. The team can jointly decide to adjust an operating agreement.	Typically, No.

PART II

WHY 10 LEADERSHIP STYLES?

Leadership is a result of an overflow of learning, adapting, and admiration for those who follow in a leadership's footsteps. It is a God-given purpose to those who accept the challenge and faithfully perform this service. Many are called, but few are chosen; those who are selected must be skillfully prepared for the meaningful task of leading others.

How many leaders does it take to screw in a light bulb? Just one (laughing!). It is a good reference to an age-old joke that smart people cannot do simple things. **But leadership is not supposed to be simple. It is complex and requires a considerable amount of thinking, sacrifice, and commitment.** For anyone endeavoring to lead, you have to find what approach allows you to be your very best. What enables one may not enable the other. Because life experiences are different, we are all shaped and molded in vastly dissimilar environments, and we have given and received diverse perspectives that have led us to this point in time. Therefore, leaders may have to experiment to ascertain which leadership approach or style properly fits their personality type. It is conceivable to believe that there should be at least one applicable leadership approach to every kind of personality. In the Myers-Brigg Personality Assessment, there are 16 potential personality types that an individual can be assessed for. In turn, there should be a similar number of choices; thereby, a personality can synchronize itself with likely leadership traits that can be classified into a leadership style. Personality is not a choice, and neither is leadership. Therefore, accurately determining which approach is best can ultimately prove life-saving or life-impeding.

PROJECT MANAGER AND LEADER

Project managers are essentially the team leader of a project team. A project manager is accountable for tasks, activities, and deliverables and works with team members to achieve a successful project outcome. Project managers create and monitor the execution of tasks by which team members will follow. The project manager's responsibility is to ensure that the customer's goals are met. This is accomplished through management and control of budget, schedule, scope, quality, resources, and performance of the project.

According to Vijay Verma, an expert in project management human resources, a good project manager acknowledges that he or she is a leader who must affect the practices of productive communication, motivation, negotiation, conflict resolution, and stress management during a project. Many experts claim that communication is the most vital of these skills. An effective project manager should be a successful communicator, able to construct and deliver a message. The Project Management Institute (PMI) says that the most valuable asset of a project manager is his ability to communicate. The components of communication consist of a sender, a message, and a receiver. A successful project manager must master all three components to adapt based on the situation. Although a project manager should be experienced and knowledgeable about tools, techniques, and methods of equal importance, he should be able to influence others when he communicates. Clear communication is a fundamental part of managing stakeholder expectations and garnering trust from everyone involved in the project team.

    The roles of project manager and leader are synonymous. Both wield power and authority that is paramount to successful organizational change. Both roles have a significant influence on the way team members perform their jobs. A project manager and leader makes judgment calls and decisions that are often final and broadly impact internal and external forces. The project manager unintentionally or intentionally sets the tone of an undertaking as he directs the tasks and activities of others. Likewise, a leader positively or negatively impacts the atmosphere by enabling team members to execute their assignments. It is frequently the role of the project manager and leader to monitor the level of performance achieved by the team and intervene with mitigation plans or adaptive strategies where appropriate.

Project leadership is a determining factor for business organizations to achieve strategic missions, goals, and objectives. Not far from the knowledge created and shared in a boardroom, project managers should be infused into the ventricles of an organization's strategic plans and activities. Using fundamental principles and practices, which include planning, scoping and risk management, a project manager offers a means for leading organizational change and policy execution. Organizations have relied largely on project management for its inclusiveness and connectivity throughout the organizational landscape. Many young leaders have built a project management background and received formal training, allowing them to coordinate, influence and implement change within their organizations. The new leadership and project management generation will be fused into one skill set, as is commonly seen today on successful projects. The project manager is accountable and responsible for all resources consumed on small and large projects. It is commonly said that a project manager is like the Chief Executive Officer of a small company. Comparably, the project manager is the chief executive of their project, often revered by team members as an indirect manager with direct impact.

In examining Bernard M. Bass's 1985 leadership theory in the project management environment, R.S. Janis (2003) found that a *laissez-faire* leadership approach produced negative outcomes. In research results, dissatisfaction and ineffectiveness were reported by surveyed study participants. On the other hand, a transformational leadership approach in project management was seen to produce the greatest positive effects on the outcome variables. A transactional approach, where the reward was reciprocated for effort, resulted in corresponding responses indicating beneficial outcomes when exhibited by project managers in their behaviors. At the conclusion of the study, Janis's results determined that the components of transformational and transitional leadership, namely those including project management leadership, would be greatly valuable to future business environments.

Offered in this book are ten leadership styles that I have empirically studied in great detail. Along my personal and professional journey, I have surmised that either one of these approaches to leadership can be the determining factor in building a loyal team of followers and partners who believe in a common purpose rather than their self-preservation. All of these styles apply to the skills and capabilities that the new generation of project managers should possess. My goal is to outline and provide descriptive analyses revealing why each of the ten leadership styles can be a potential vehicle for a project manager. The journey begins when a project manager makes a choice about what type of leader he or she would like to be. Then, using the common characteristics and attributes of the style should make it easier for a leader who shares comparable personality traits.

WHY 10 LEADERSHIP STYLES

Future generations of project managers should enjoy this exciting opportunity to learn from the next ten chapters filled with useful facts, analogies and life stories that illuminate your potential for becoming a highly effective leader.

10 Leadership Styles for Highly Effective Project Managers:

- Project
- Skills
- Style
- Situational
- Path-Goal
- Continency
- Emotional
- Christian
- Servant
- Transformational

1 PROJECT PROFESSIONAL LEADERSHIP STYLE

Project professional leaders often major in the intricacies of plan-driven approaches where the tasks of the project drive expectations. These leaders are focused on challenging projects that require vital skills to manage people and their work. Professionals operating in diverse environments and cultures must foresee the necessity to acquire knowledge and skills that go beyond management but endeavors to energize people and their work. The Project Management Institute (PMI) says that project managers should be able to adjust and adapt to disparate situations to successfully accommodate the changes and challenges involved in a typical project. Critical project challenges often include turbulent issues with people's behavior. However, the complexity of work and its contribution to a person's behavior should be accounted for. **Understanding the emotions of a team member can assist project managers with the 2-fold priority they often navigate: team member performance and getting the work done.**

How can Project Management be defined? A project is a temporary endeavor that has a definite beginning and end that is designed to accomplish a specific goal (pmi.org). A project can be constrained by a certain budget and the number of days required to complete it in order to meet an objective. Project managers are organized, goal-oriented professionals who use passion, creativity, and collaboration to design projects that are destined for success (pmi.org). Project management is comprised of professional tools, techniques, and methodologies used for the purposes of managing the tasks, activities, and resources involved in a project (Arora & Baronikian, 2013). Project management also consists of professional procedures that ensure the accurate identification, control, and reporting of an initiative's health. A project's health can be measured based on the severity of risks, spending rate and tasks completed. When the health of a project is below an acceptable level, measures to mitigate risks can be taken. If a project is spending more money than originally intended by the team, measures can be taken to slow the burn rate. Similarly, delays in the tasks and activities to be completed can be mitigated through project management practices that bring the schedule in line with expectations.

Importance of Project Management. The value of project management cannot be overstated. Researchers, scholars, and practitioners have collected a multitude of empirical data to support the value of formal project management (Nelson, 2014; Wills, 2015; Yeager, 2017). The tools, methods, and processes involved in *projectizing* work have proven to be beneficial in the implementation of change. With general acceptance of common and standard practices across the business spectrum, project management is a viable part of most industries. According to project managers questioned in the *Earning Power: Project Management Salary Survey* (2021, 12 ed.), many workers have formal titles and roles within their industries. As depicted in Table 2, survey results demonstrate the broad range of industries in which project managers are formally recognized.

Table 2 Industries Where Project Managers Work January (2021)

INDUSTRY	N=	PERCENT	25TH PERCENTILE	MEDIAN	75TH PERCENTILE	MEAN
Aerospace	3	*	-	-	-	-
Business Services	2	*	-	-	-	-
Construction	86	10%	118,000	130,000	168,500	148,487
Consulting	60	7%	122,000	160,500	197,250	163,051
Engineering	85	10%	113,292	140,000	180,000	147,094
Financial Services	59	7%	125,000	165,000	193,000	168,944
Food and Beverage	6	1%	-	-	-	-
Government	84	9%	120,000	149,067	194,500	158,932
Healthcare	30	3%	106,750	148,000	180,938	148,744
Information Technology	210	24%	120,000	142,000	170,484	150,579
Insurance	8	1%	-	-	-	-
Legal	1	*	-	-	-	-
Manufacturing	29	3%	107,000	125,000	154,172	134,650
Pharmaceuticals	12	1%	121,250	138,750	158,750	138,125
Real Estate	5	1%	-	-	-	-
Resources (Agriculture, Mining, etc.)	55	6%	141,973	174,000	210,000	183,569
Telecommunications	69	8%	127,500	150,000	185,000	150,398
Training/Education	12	1%	124,203	135,000	192,500	155,509
Utility	30	3%	99,000	137,000	160,750	133,834
Other	44	5%	130,000	150,000	178,125	157,482

Note: Reprinted from *Earning Power: Project Management Salary Survey* from Project Management Institute Copyright 2021 by PMI Publications.

In addition to broad industry support of the importance of project management, internal departments within companies have acknowledged the need for project managers to oversee critical implementation of change. From the department of Human Resources to Sales & Marketing, a project manager can be found to be instrumental in leading teams in the pursuit of critical and complex efforts that require professional expertise (Hersey & Blanchard, 1988). As depicted in the table below, the results of the *Earning Power: Project Management Salary Survey* (2021) show respondents who have formal positions as project managers in various functional departments of the organization (see Table 3). Organizations are utilizing project methodologies to ensure company goals and objectives are being met. Indicative of well-managed projects, organizations also acknowledge the people leadership and human resource management benefits of executing work through the establishment of a formal project. Businesses that are significantly impacted by unplanned risks appropriately relegate management of key initiatives to project management as a sole practice to mitigate problematic change. Through the use of tools, techniques and a generally accepted methodology, organizations see the advantages of allowing project management to implement strategic directives.

Table 3 Departments Where Project Managers Work (2021)

DEPARTMENT	N=	PERCENT	25TH PERCENTILE	MEDIAN	75TH PERCENTILE	MEAN
Administration/General Management	50	%	110,000	133,500	192,500	151,545
Consulting	72	8%	120,000	148,000	190,000	157,740
Customer Service/Public Relations	3	*	-	-	-	-
Engineering	93	10%	110,000	130,000	168,500	145,925
Finance	11	1%	120,000	135,000	180,000	169,727
Human Resources	2	*	-	-	-	-
Information Technology/Information Systems	203	23%	125,000	150,000	180,000	156,996
Operations/Manufacturing	38	4%	119,750	141,202	185,875	151,819
Project Management Department or PMO	339	38%	122,000	150,000	80,000	155,807
Quality Management	8	1%	-	-	-	-
Research and Development	15	2%	110,000	125,000	145,000	127,367
Sales/Marketing	10	1%	99,500	126,750	176,250	131,312
Supply Chain Management/Logistics	10	1%	128,739	160,000	189,866	154,781
Training/Education	5	1%	-	-	-	-
Other	31	3%	110,000	139,808	180,000	149,998

Annualized Salary by Department

Note: Reprinted from *Earning Power: Project Management Salary Survey* from Project Management Institute Copyright 2021 by PMI Publications.

2 SKILLS-BASED LEADERSHIP STYLE

The skills-based leadership approach suggests that behavior and ability can be learned and practiced. In 2010, leadership expert Larry Spears theorized that leadership skills could be taught and were not necessarily a product of personality or trait. In their ground-breaking edition of *The Leadership Challenge* (2007), James Kouzes and Barry Posner also explained that the practice of good leadership could be a learned skill. Though leaders come from different backgrounds with varying degrees of education, each can improve. The skills approach highlights the relationship between knowledge, skills (capability) and performance. Leaders must continually learn new skills and remain on a careful path of self-renewal where they gainfully increase their maturity and ability to address challenges successfully. While engaging in varying experiences, a good leader can acquire new skills from every personal and professional interaction.

Former Apple CEO Steve Jobs has been seen as one of the most successful business leaders of his generation, ultimately transforming the lives of people worldwide. Jobs exhibited all three skills-based model components: knowledge, skills, and performance. With multiple technology innovations to his credit, Jobs challenged the existing science and practitioners to think beyond their capacity and envision new possibilities. A good leader has an invaluable toolbox containing an assortment of techniques that can be applied to any situation after reaching a certain level of adequacy and achieving good results; innovative leaders look for opportunities to innovate. Leaders like Jobs understand that the future brings about new challenges to be overcome. **Leaders must be on a continuum of skills learning and collaboration to ensure new challenges are addressed.**

A project manager could make good use of the skills approach. Being that project managers are not innate leaders, they, too, must seek ways to increase leadership prowess through the acquisition of new skills, techniques, and knowledge. Continuous engagement in forms of ongoing professional development is a highly regarded strength among effective project managers.

3 STYLE LEADERSHIP APPROACH

Leaders have strengths and weaknesses that allow them to perform better in one situation or another. In 2010, Susan D. Little developed a doctoral dissertation that compared leaders' self-perceptions of their behavior, orientation/style, and managerial and leadership effectiveness with the perceptions expressed by their supervisors, peers, and subordinates. To measure the results, Little relied on Bolman and Deal's *Leadership Orientation Instrument-Self (LOI-Self)* to assess individual leaders' self-perceptions and the *Leadership Orientation Instrument-Other (LOI-Other)*. The analysis was used to gauge the perceptions of leaders' supervisors, peers, and subordinates. The results were that leaders rated themselves higher than others. In effect, one's leadership style was seen as effective at a higher percentage of times above the perception of others. It is not

SKILLS-BASED LEADERSHIP STYLE

often that a leader's perception of himself matches that of his subordinates.

Although an effective "leader-match" with varying types of teams, groups and followers can be difficult to arrange, here is a fictitious example of a *positive* result:

An example of a leader with effective Style leadership characteristics can be seen in the case of Bill Braski. Braski is a police lieutenant working in the Chicago Southland Precinct. He supervises the activities of two police squads that patrol the streets of Southland daily. Police officers who work in this volatile environment are unique in their tolerance for being at risk of danger; therefore, different standards apply to their behavior in dealing with unpredictable situations. Braski's style of people management is flexible, accommodating, and attentive to special needs. His style is more effective when leading his police squads in this environment rather than a style that requires a rigid process.

Here is a fictitious example of a *negative* result from a "leader-match" that was not effective when matched up with a team:

An example of a leader who leads with unproductive Style characteristics is Eunice Fairchild who works as Chief of Emergency Care in the ICU at Mercy Hospital in Boston,

Massachusetts. Her leadership style incorporates extreme sensitivity to others and a desire to make everyone happy. In a hospital ward filled with fast-moving doctors, nurses and medical personnel, there is often a lack of sensitivity. In the position of leader over emergency services, Fairchild's persistent sympathy overreaches the boundaries of expressing concern. It often distracts her staff from making timely decisions concerning emergency care towards patients. As a leader, Fairchild is less effective given this environment where her staff requires more expediency over carefulness.

The Style approach to leadership is based on self-perception and behavior (Fiedler & Garcia, 1987). **Style is often natural and organic for a leader in an appropriate situation.** This approach suggests that leadership is categorized into two general kinds of behavior: task-oriented behavior and relationship-oriented behavior (McCaffery, 2004). Task-oriented behavior seeks to guide constituents or followers down the path of completing their goals and objectives. Relationship-oriented behavior enables a leader to appeal to the followers' comfortability in a certain situation. The focus is on what Style approach a leader uses to influence followers and how they act within the environment (Northouse, 2007). Prominent leadership theorists and practitioners advocate the superior capabilities of a style approach leader as ideal in solving leader-follower challenges that are prevalent in varying environments.

In Ohio State and the University of Michigan studies, Robert Blake and Jane Mouton (1964) examined leadership styles based on the variable of behavior. As a result of the study, the researchers developed a leadership grid that focuses on leaders' concern for people (relationships) versus production (tasks). By examining one's attributes from the grid, Blake and Mouton were able to identify when the behavior of a leader constituted more prevalence than another. The following grid (figure 1) gives a picture of two dimensions of leadership behavior, **relationship orientation** (people's needs get priority) on the y-axis and **task orientation** (concerned with production) on the x-axis, with each size having a range graded from a low of '1' to a high of '9', resulting in 81 unique positions where a leader's style may be depicted.

SKILLS-BASED LEADERSHIP STYLE

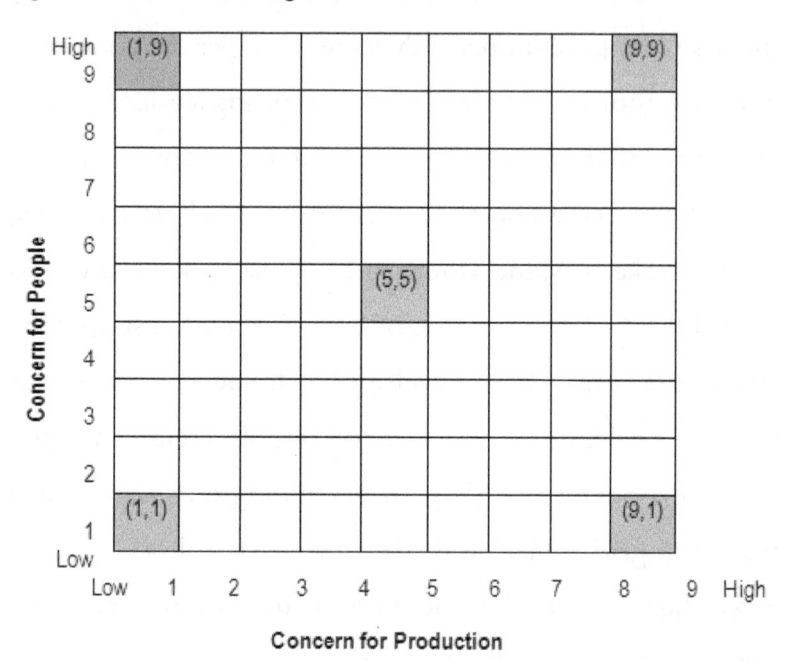

Figure 1. The New Management Grid

[Management Grid showing Concern for People (y-axis, Low 1 to High 9) vs Concern for Production (x-axis, Low 1 to High 9), with labeled points: (1,9) at top-left, (9,9) at top-right, (5,5) at center, (1,1) at bottom-left, (9,1) at bottom-right]

The five resulting leadership styles are as defined in the Management Study Guide for the Grid (Juneja, 2013):

- **Impoverished Management (1, 1):** Managers with this approach are low on both dimensions and exercise minimum effort to get the work done by subordinates. The leader has low concern for employee satisfaction and work deadlines; as a result, disharmony and disorganization prevail within the organization. The leaders are termed ineffective, wherein their action merely aims to preserve jobs and seniority.

SKILLS-BASED LEADERSHIP STYLE

- **Task Management (9, 1):** Also called dictatorial or perish style. Here, leaders are more concerned about production and less concerned about people. The style is based on Douglas McGregor's Theory of X. The employees' needs are not taken care of, and they are simply a means to an end. The leader believes that efficiency can result only through proper organization of work systems and by eliminating people wherever possible. Such a style can increase the organisation's output in the short run, but high labour turnover is inevitable due to strict policies and procedures.

- **Middle-of-the-Road (5, 5):** This is basically a compromising style wherein the leader tries to balance the company's goals and people's needs. The leader does not push the boundaries of achievement, resulting in an average performance for the organization. Here, neither employee nor production needs are fully met.

- **Country Club (1, 9):** This is a collegial style characterized by low task and high people orientation where the leader gives thoughtful attention to the needs of people, thus providing them with a friendly and comfortable environment. The leader feels that such treatment with employees will lead to self-motivation and will find people working hard on their own. However, a low focus on tasks can hamper production and lead to questionable results.

- **Team Management (9, 9):** Characterized by high people and task focus, the style is based on Douglas McGregor's Theory of Y and has been termed as the most effective style according to Blake and Mouton. The leader feels that empowerment, commitment, trust, and respect are the key elements in creating a team atmosphere which will automatically result in high employee satisfaction and production.

4 SITUATIONAL LEADERSHIP STYLE

High-achieving organizations are known for addressing and resolving challenging problems by utilizing the appropriate leadership approach to motivate team members to do their best. The widely researched approach of situational leadership employs effective tactics applicable to any given scenario (Hersey, 1985). **Competent and productive situational leaders deal in fluctuating environments that often contend with change. These resourceful leaders can reframe and adapt their style to meet the needs of the organization and their followers.** The following model, developed by Blanchard and Hersey in 1960, explains the correlation between leadership styles (i.e., directing, supporting, delegating, coaching) and the development levels of subordinates in a simple grid shown in Figure 2 (Situational Leadership Model, 1960):

Figure 2. Situational leadership model

Directing Leaders define the roles and tasks of the 'follower', and supervise them closely. Decisions are made by the leader and announced, so communication is largely one-way.
Coaching Leaders still define roles and tasks, but seeks ideas and suggestions from the follower. Decisions remain the leader's prerogative, but communication is much more two-way.
Supporting Leaders pass day-to-day decisions, such as task allocation and processes, to the follower. The leader facilitates and takes part in decisions, but control is with the follower.
Delegating Leaders are still involved in decisions and problem-solving, but control is with the follower. The follower decides when and how the leader will be involved.

	Supportive Behaviour	
	SUPPORTING (S3)	COACHING (S2)
	DELEGATING (S4)	DIRECTING (S1)

− Directive Behaviour +

In a 2010 study, Margaret R. Lee calls situational leadership an "e-leadership" style because it is commonly used on virtual projects where teams are geographically dispersed. In her research, Lee used concurrent triangulation in a mixed methods study to investigate how and to what degree situational leadership characteristics, such as effectiveness and flexibility, affect the success of virtual projects. The *Leadership Behavioral Analysis II-Self (LABII-Self)* was used to survey a group of Project Management Professionals (PMP) to evaluate their leadership characteristics. The results showed that there were no project managers who had higher or lower effectiveness and flexibility scores in correlation with the project manager's virtual project success scores. In her

SITUATIONAL LEADERSHIP STYLE

qualitative explanation, more discussion and research were recommended since the study of situational leadership could not definitively correlate to virtual project management.

The relationship between a situational leader and their team holds stark correlations. The relationship is seminal and impactful to the success of the other. A positive example of a situational leader who has been influenced equally by the team is former National Basketball Association (NBA) player Michael Jordan. Jordan accumulated six NBA Championship trophies in legendary fashion while starring on mediocre teams. His ability to utilize the average talent on his team was not immediately evident; however, Jordan became a more mature leader with time and adapted to a situation that surrounded him with average talent. Jordan capitalized off the strengths of the players around him while catapulting himself onto stardom. Jordan's true talent was situational leadership.

Former NBA player Allen Iverson is an example of a *negative* situational leader. Unlike Jordan, he could not operate successfully in a less-than-ideal situation. He, too, had an unimpressive cast of team members surrounding him. However, Iverson failed to catalyze their talent during his tenure in the NBA. To the disappointment of five NBA teams for whom Iverson was the leader, he was never able to guide them to a championship as Jordan successfully achieved.

Of all the approaches, situational leadership is perhaps the most popular amongst project managers in various industries. The **Project Management Institute (PMI) says that project managers should be able to adjust and adapt to disparate situations to successfully accommodate the changes and challenges involved in a typical project (pmi.org).** Regardless of the level of complexity, cost or scope, most projects experience requirements that change mid-stream. Moreover, a highly effective project manager must understand how to modify work plans, maneuver resources, and reconcile any lost benefits to the project due to the occurrence of unexpected risks. A project manager must possess flexibility and the ability to adapt to situations that are progressively culminating.

5 PATH-GOAL LEADERSHIP STYLE

Like psychodynamic leadership, path-goal leadership is a theory about how leaders motivate subordinates to accomplish designated goals. According to the theory, subordinates are primarily motivated when they believe they are competent and can perform the tasks required to achieve the specific goals of their job. **The path-goal leader is charged with finding motivating tactics for each subordinate and offering outcomes that are valuable to them.** Robert J. House and Terrace R. Mitchell (1974, p. 81-97) refer to this exchange of motivation for a beneficial outcome as a "payoff":

Leadership generates motivation when it increases the number and kinds of payoffs that subordinates receive from their work. Leadership also motivates when it makes the *path to the goal clear* and easy to travel through coaching and direction, removing obstacles and roadblocks to attaining the goal and making the work more personally satisfying.

A 1983 study conducted by Cornelius J. Mes found that elementary school principals may consider practicing path-goal leadership based on beneficial responses from teachers who displayed higher job satisfaction. This study was done in an educational setting to determine the applicability of the path-goal theory for predicting leader behavior/teacher job satisfaction. A *Leadership Behavior Description Questionnaire XII (LBDQ XII)* was used to measure leadership behavior in two ways: structure and behavior. Intrinsic, extrinsic, and general job satisfaction was measured by a Description Index (JDI). A Likert scale was used to determine leader effectiveness. As demonstrated by the elementary school principals in the study, the path-goal approach of leadership displayed behaviors and characteristics that generated a positive effect on subordinates and/or followers.

In corporate America, business leaders are hired to increase profit, reduce costs, and improve market penetration. Former Hewlett Packard (HP) CEO Carly Fiorina is an example of a Fortune 500 business leader who reached a significant level of accomplishment. Unfortunately, her keen sense of profitable decision-making did not result in immediate success for HP. After she was terminated from the CEO position, the company began to see the rewards of the large corporate changes she had started. Inevitably, goal-driven leaders like Fiorina understand the steps that need to be taken to reach success. This type of leader can be somewhat obsessive or directive in their leadership style. A leader employing a directive style expects his or her subordinates to follow clear and concise compliance with instructions to meet expectations. In this respect, both obsessive and directive styles match up well. Unfortunately, the direct approach can result in unintended results due to a lack of emotional interaction and relationship building.

Motivation is a constant component of the path-goal style of leadership. However, the predominant characteristic is that of a task-driven manager. In project management, path-goal leadership is often an overwhelmingly reliant skill. Project managers determine the scope, schedule, and cost and build a work plan to accomplish the project's goals. The project plan consists of tasks and activities that are closely monitored and tracked. Indirectly, the project manager is accountable for resources assigned to the project even

PATH-GOAL LEADERSHIP STYLE

though they are normally not direct reports. Therefore, a project manager must be very effective at motivating the team to focus keenly on the project's goals, which is the essence of successful path-goal management.

6 CONTINGENCY LEADERSHIP STYLE

Contingency leadership was formulated to get leaders in a "matching" situation that fit well with their aptitude and capabilities. Leaders have strengths and weaknesses that allow them to be more valuable in one job over another. According to prominent theorists, the contingency approach says that certain leaders cannot be effective in the wrong situations (Fiedler & Garcia, 1987). They contend that a "leader-match" factor is involved in organizational leadership effectiveness.

Some variables contend with the effect by which contingency leadership can be applied. Contingency theorist Christian Bach defines uncertainty and environment as considerable variables by which outcomes can be influenced. Other factors include organizational strategy, technology, and size of the organization. These variables can contribute to the success or failure of properly leading a high-performance organization. As a result, the organization forms itself around the effectiveness of each contingency utilized in organizational performance. Likewise, **the leadership strategy for a contingency approach is to match leaders to variables in which they can be effective in providing influence.** When the necessary variables are affirmed, leaders affect organizational behavior and enable norms, culture, and customs inherent within the community to be preserved.

In project management, contingency leadership can be utilized to impact a project that is in the ditch. In a common example, a project manager is placed in the role because of a unique skill set in this area. To curtail potential failures of a complex initiative, management assigns a project manager because of their leadership style that highly emphasises tasks and interpersonal relationships. Variables of the organization (i.e., environment, technology, size) are matched to the right project manager with a proven ability to be effective in the situation. Contingency leadership is a productive measure in project management because it emphasizes getting project managers in a "matching" situation. As leaders, project managers have strengths and weaknesses that allow them to be better in one organizational environment over another.

7 EMOTIONAL INTELLIGENCE LEADERSHIP STYLE

Commercialized by Daniel Goleman in 1995, emotional intelligence (EI) took prominent flight amongst the archives of leadership approaches. Generally dealing with an admonition of self-evaluation, EI also ventures to capture the ability of a leader to relate to others. The term "emotional intelligence" appears to be first used in a 1983 doctoral thesis attributed to Wayne Payne in his study of emotions. However, as early as 1964, studies were published that reflected the identification of emotional intelligence (Beldoch, 1964). Leaders utilize EI to effectively understand their feelings appropriately. More importantly, leaders recognize the feelings and behavior of others so that necessary adjustments can be made to achieve the organisation's goals.

Individual emotional states can be observed and interpreted through various behaviors, including facial expression, voice tone, and physical movement. Several studies conducted by theorists have found that certain behaviors indicate one's feelings, allowing observers to recognize positive and negative effects. EI provides a science whereby the study of personal emotions and relationships can be labeled and adjusted to create better outcomes. Before the significant study of EI, the focus of emotional meaning was primarily on labeling feelings. As a science, EI is now used in training others to discern and adjust behaviors that negatively impact communications within relationships and team dynamics.

Many leaders find displeasure in revealing their emotional side. Depending on the environment, no one wants to avail their feelings to the scrutiny of their peers' observations. However, Goleman suggests that a transparent discussion where the leader and team members disclose their emotions will drive empathy and a shared commitment around values that apply to everyone. Essentially, **EI leaders can be identified as leaders who are aware of personal and social competencies that impact their ability to motivate themselves and their followers.** Often defined as the ability to monitor one's own and other people's emotions, EI is a prolific skill that is not used enough in the workforce. Three models generally instruct EI, using trait, mixed and ability. Psychologists Peter Salovey and John Mayer were the first to coin the phrase "emotional intelligence" in 1990, using these three models to offer theorists and practitioners a method by which EI should be interpreted and applied in corporate and social environments.

TRAIT MODEL OF EMOTIONAL INTELLIGENCE.

The trait model includes behavioral dispositions and self-perceived abilities. Charismatic leaders can consistently possess traits of self-monitoring, engagement in impression management, motivation to attain social power, and motivation to achieve self-actualization. Here, we recognise the inextricable link between trait leadership and charismatic behavior. As a trait and transformational leader, the first Black South African president, Nelson Mandela, captured a nation's anxiety, turmoil, and strife through letters and speeches. While imprisoned, Mandela inspired both inmates and guards to ascend to a higher level of respect and servitude towards the betterment of humankind and civility. Mandela exemplified an understanding of behavioral dispositions and self-perceived abilities often found in practitioners of the trait model in various environments.

ABILITY MODEL OF EMOTIONAL INTELLIGENCE.

The ability model focuses on individual ability to process emotional information and use it to traverse social conditions. The model tests individuals for EI by assigning tasks that evaluate separate abilities: perception, use, understanding and management of emotions. Known as an EI-centric leader, eBay CEO John Donahoe was the subject of many widely shared articles for his business exploits. With a grand sense of self-direction, Donahoe transformed eBay's lacklustre performance in the fast-paced digital age into a competitive 21st-century player. Donahoe engineered a culture of corporate loyalty by listening and acting on a social agenda that captured deep loyalty in the company. The capacity to apprehend emotional concerns relative to individual needs and converge with corporate goals is a key component of the ability model.

MIXED MODEL OF EMOTIONAL INTELLIGENCE.

The mixed model is a combination of trait & ability models. Essentially, trait and ability models are mixed

EMOTIONAL INTELLIGENCE LEADERSHIP STYLE

to take advantage of EI created by mental ability and evaluated by performance tests and EI defined by traits primarily measured by self-perception. Full utilization of EI is the capability to look inwardly and outwardly at one's behavior and the emotional effect on others. Furthermore, the efficiency of how an individual can promote relationship building using emotional connections is an indication of superior use of EI.

Leaders who build loyal relationships in a diverse social environment are versed in the EI approach. Ultimately, leaders who do not understand or perceive the emotions of others fail to meet the needs of their constituents. The 2016 Presidential candidate, Donald Trump, embodied leadership qualities that dissuaded an acknowledgment of appeasement towards the goals of others. As a self-declared "solo candidate", Trump repeatedly asserted that he would listen to his advice and was not interested in the counsel of others. In a 2016 television interview on CNN, Trump admitted that he did not trust anyone. Based on the success of past presidential campaigns, candidates needed to demonstrate an overwhelming recognition of the needs of others. In Trump's case, he did the opposite by outlining his personal goals and enlisting those who would be loyal to help him achieve them. This scheme of self-promotion and preservation created an unexpected relationship between Trump and his constituents, offering a unique example of how counter-cultural elements can break proven rules.

8 CHRISTIAN LEADERSHIP STYLE

In government, officials in traditional leadership positions are appointed or elected to office to manage cities, states, and countries. Traditional leaders are typically chosen by the electorate based on what they have promised to do after winning the election. Even with the best of intentions, many of these leaders go on to perform in a self-serving way that increases their personal wealth, power, and opportunities for higher office. They work on building a reputation that will help them win the next election. In addition to constantly campaigning for the next term's election, traditional leaders continually fundraise by promising to fix the problems of unwitting donors.

In contrast to the traditionally elected leader, a Christian leader operates upon the premise of a greater purpose connected to a divine nature, which is quite the opposite of one who is elected. In Philippians 2:7 (KJV), Paul writes that Jesus "made himself of no reputation." This is because Jesus did not want any of the glory to come to himself but to God for all the good deeds he would do during his ministry. Acts 10:38 (NIV) states, "God anointed Jesus of Nazareth with the Holy Spirit and power, and how he went around doing good and healing all who were under the power of the devil because God was with him." By intent, Jesus designated his life to be of no concern with prestige, promotion, value, or commodity. Likewise, a Christian leader should be of the same constitution: one who is above reproach, sober-minded, self-controlled, respectable, hospitable, and able to teach (I Tim 3:2, NIV).

In organizational leadership, Christian leaders must take a critical look at their group and see what is wrong or right. **A Christian leader should ascribe to looking at the organization at arm's length to enable the ability to focus on the right thing. Sometimes, this leads to a path of taking a step in the opposite direction to avoid self-serving choices that run counter to the organization's goals and values.** In his 2010 book titled *Steward Leader,* R. Scott Rodin claims that a Christian leader's reflection should not only encompass thoughts of how church members may perceive actions but also how God sees them. A Christian leader is concerned with his or her spiritual being and that of others in conjunction with a personal relationship with God. New questions that should be added to reflective thinking for aspiring Christian leaders are, "Does this decision demonstrate the love of God?" "Am I accomplishing my goal of building a relationship with my people by doing this?" "Is this a self-serving response if I address this situation this way?" Christian leaders must ensure that they are leading the process freely and joyfully as caretakers of the church within the community. Ultimately, a Christian leader's resolve should be that this is God's community, not his or hers.

By illustrating the real heart of God through emulating His image, Christian leaders also have an important role to play in secular environments. As a witness to the power of a divine God, Christian leaders can influence the removal of the negativity in their environment and replace it with love, care, and adoration. When God puts Christians in team leadership positions in the world, there is a substantial opportunity to influence team members.

GODLY LEADERSHIP

The scripture states, "Without counsel, plans fail, but with many advisers, they succeed" (Proverbs 15:22, ESV). Leaders should pay careful attention and consider the message that suggests that counselors should be *plural*, not just one. It is evident that wrong counsel can defeat the purpose of seeking counsel. However, many counselors can provide objective opinions and allow a person to determine the best decision that aligns with God's word. Many advisors may be necessary for sound judgment or decision-making. If a leader is to appeal to the word of God for direction in reducing the anxiety and concern involved in the decision-making process, leaders would perhaps study the book of Proverbs. Proverbs 3:5-6 (ESV) states, "Trust in the Lord with all your heart, and do not lean on your own understanding. In all your ways acknowledge him, and he will make straight your paths." Within this translation of scripture, we can embellish that God does not desire leaders to rely on themselves or others for direction, but leaders should consider God's way and allow them to make the way clear. Further principles in the word of God instruct leaders to seek counsel from other godly leaders.

Clearly, in the Scriptures, leaders have experienced great success by becoming imitators of their predecessors. Many of them replaced their predecessors, assuming the assignment given by God and continuing to implement God's ultimate will. In the example of Hosea, he was a contemporary of Isaiah and Amos. Hosea prophesized the destruction of the land of Israel during a prosperous time in the nation (Hosea 1:1 ESV). As with his predecessors, Hosea was given the command by God to warn, describe and communicate the damnation of the land if the Israelites did not turn from ungodly ways. Willfully, Hosea started as a young preacher and continued to admonish the prophets that came before him. Through carefully observing his predecessors, he would become a leader in his own right.

GOOD JUDGMENT

The primary job of a good leader is to make good judgment calls that affect others. **Good decision-making ability is the essence of effective leadership.** Leaders should be able to make good judgment calls that impact the profit margin, enhance processes, and improve the environment to succeed. One key reason leaders fail is that they do not involve other people in decision-making. There is a "go it alone" complex that permeates many of today's leaders. Some leaders are consumed with past experiences where a certain approach worked very well in another organization. However, in their current organization, the approach does not work. The leader may ask, "What changed?" Undoubtedly, it is the environment that has changed. In turn, leaders must be comfortable with engaging new behavioral approaches wherever they go.

According to EI expert Daniel Goleman, a *current* is the object that precedes an organization's decision-making and emotional framework. Organizational *currents* are the feelings transmitted on a group level and offer leaders an opportunity to impact the group with targeted, dynamic tactics. Reading the organization *currents* that travel via spoken and unspoken communication methods is important for emotionally intelligent leaders. The result is an organization with a resonance that ultimately carries these feelings into the service of the customers. The bottom line of an organization can shift when workers are providing service that is enthusiastic, upbeat, and ready to go to great lengths to please the customers. As *currents* apply to good decision-making, a leader should have enough information to make a good judgment call. Unfortunately, the *currents* of information may not be material or intelligible but apply to a negative feeling or thought if the wrong decision is made. Therefore, a leader's strategy must be to ascertain the opinions of all he or she trusts in the matter and then formulate the best decision affecting everyone involved.

9 SERVANT LEADERSHIP STYLE

Robert Greenleaf provides a frequently referenced definition of servant leadership: "(Servant Leadership) begins with the natural feeling that one wants to serve, to serve *first*. Then conscious choice brings one to aspire to lead... The difference manifests itself in the care taken by the servant: first to make sure that other people's highest priority needs are being served."

This idea agrees with contemporary thinkers who also place primary emphasis on the team members. The consensus is that the development of each team member is essential to the productivity of an organization. Servant leadership can seem natural for some who practice it, but it can also be a learned skill for others. In his 2010 book titled *Servant Leadership and Robert K. Greenleaf's Legacy*, Larry Spears characterizes a servant leader by ten points:

active listening, empathy, healing, awareness, persuasion, conceptualization, foresight, stewardship, commitment to growth, and community building. My doctoral dissertation focused on Spear's ten points of servant leadership and observed whether positive project success outcomes could reflect a project manager's use of them. The empirical study surveyed 49 project managers who worked in the technology domain, asking questions that measured the degree of servant leadership emulated in successful projects.

Author Bill Flint defines trained servant leaders as "men and women who bring their purpose, passion, and character, and when combined with God-given skills and abilities for leadership, bring out the best in people, helping a business to develop and implement a sustainable process for success." In any business domain or industry, a leader can be identified as one who makes people and the business successful. **Albeit, the distinguishing characteristic of the successful servant leader from any other style of leadership is that he measures success against how well he cared for people**. In popular management practices, the benefit or success of the people is rarely a priority. In businesses involving shareholders and owners, the singular measurement of success is increased share value or wealth ownership. Contrastingly, a servant leader believes that everyone's growth and increase in value can be realized: leaders, followers, and business. This leadership style is concerned with building relationships that revolve around trust and respect to impact the lives of their teammates beyond work but personally. Even though employees normally spend more time at work than at home, servant leaders are consistently aware and conscious of personal values and beliefs shared with followers.

Defined as one who is not self-serving, the *steward leader* closely resembles the servant leader. The steward leader is not looking for the validation of his own actions or working to improve his reputation through acts of grandeur or self-preservation. In comparison, the servant leader is concerned with psychological and physical synchronization and less about business platitudes. A servant leader cannot build his or her values and beliefs on something other than principles, or else he or she is going to fail. Regardless of the type of industry, businesses fail due to fallen leadership who may have had good ideas. Still, their foundations were proceeded by selfish intentions or self-serving personal agendas.

In contrast to selfish & self-serving leadership, servant

leadership offers a remedy for these crisis-producing leaders. Often, a potential servant leader will stumble down a path of demise even with the best of intentions of inspiring, caring for, and motivating others to succeed. To morph this inevitable problem, servant leaders should seek training, mentoring, and coaching to be successful.

Leaders in a professional environment who emulate people-first characteristics would be referred to as servant leadership. One example is Leslie Hurdon, a Director of Operations at BNB Bank. While managing several ethnically diverse groups, Hurdon determined that each required a different type of leadership to accommodate their needs. For example, her Indian employees are not publicly expressive. They tend to avoid confrontation and approaching management on job challenges that impact them personally. Indian employees are more likely to handle a problem within their group rather than bring it to management. To share the goals and ideas of this cultural group, Hurdon encouraged direct communications and a policy that reassured everyone that they had access to management. Hurdon energized her policy by engaging her employees in open and friendly conversation, often recognising them individually. Hurdon asserted that management should not just recognize employees for performing at a high level; management should commend employees whenever possible and frequently.

An example of failing to lead others with a servant approach is the disgraced CEO of Volkswagen, Martin Winterkorn. In 2015, he resigned over allegations that he knowingly allowed false emissions testing to be performed on vehicles. The revelation was amidst a failed leadership tenure where relationships with employees were tumultuous. Contrary to servant leadership, where the emphasis is placed on the benefit and improvement of others, Winterkorn publicly blasted employees to secure contrition to his standard of perfection. The ex-CEO was known to walk the vehicle factory floor performing on-the-spot examinations that lower-level associates were tasked to do to personify a perfective culture. However, the attitude never rolled downward to staff members. The shared needs of his employees being met were not the priority on Winterkorn's list of objectives. Ultimately, he failed at leading people and, therefore, could not successfully lead the company. Servant leadership aspires to place focus on the follower, not the leader. Those who learn to practice servant leadership must reverse their thinking on what it takes to be successful in the workplace.

PRINCIPLES OF SERVANT LEADERSHIP

Serving and leading are mostly intuition-based concepts, according to Greenleaf. This sentiment contributes to the thought that one is born with innate sensitivity and partialities to be a servant to others. **Through natural inclinations, certain people understand the underlying workings of people and how their emotions affect what they do. A servant leader espouses to maintain an organic belief and value system given by God to share with others.** This principle of natural intuition is not teachable but is inherently a characteristic of servant leadership in which further development can be learned. Serving others through leadership is a mandate. In Matthew 20 (NLT), Jesus says, "Whoever wants to be a leader among you must be your servant, and whoever wants to be first among you must become your slave. For even the Son of Man came not to be served but to serve others and to give his life as a ransom for many." As a response, potential leaders should accept the mandate as a chief principle to follow as they develop into successful servants who lead.

SERVANT LEADERS ARE EMOTIONALLY INTELLIGENT

A servant leader develops a sense of social awareness by becoming accountable and responsible for the people and the environment around him. A major principle of the commensurate servant leader is that he is emotionally intelligent. He is concerned with his actions and the actions of others that impact culture. He understands the *social contract* that former New York Mayor Rudy Giuliani refers to as a "two-way street" where each party is obligated to exchange beliefs and values that make everyone successful.

In addition to the social domain, a servant leader is also adept to the second area of emotional intelligence (EI) competencies referred to as the *personal domain*. The personal domain of EI has to do with the way a person manages his emotions. Being self-aware is the primary area of competence in the personal domain. To exert confidence as a leader, he must be aware of how his feelings affect him in every situation. Since emotions carry a high degree of weight that can trigger physical or mental changes in people, emotions must be recognized by the leader and evaluated for strengths or weaknesses. Self-aware people typically find time to reflect inwardly and think about choices made. They often have a guiding philosophy or spiritual conviction that enables their awareness of who they are and their capabilities. Author Bill Flint reasons that this consciousness of spiritual purpose is a natural inclination that is God-inspired, unimpeded by self-interest or individual biases. In this path of thinking, a leader is astute in his message to followers. Bearing confidence, he can be a contagion that trickles down to followers from a leader who continually communicates his transcendent care for the team. On high-performance teams, there is an extraordinary degree of confidence in that people know what they are doing to complete tasks. Even when there are setbacks and surprises that alter the timeline and pressure people to perform tasks in record time, a self-aware person has positive feelings about the team's talent to get the work done. Both the social and personal domains are of equal importance to the success of the servant leader.

SERVANT LEADERSHIP IN BUSINESS

The demand for servant leaders in businesses has not been fully realized yet. Prevalently, transformational leadership is the style by which many organizations are leaning towards seeking training for their leaders. This is due to popular research and studies indicating how successful transformational leaders have been in influencing and motivating others to do more than they were initially capable of performing. However, Flint advises that servant leadership is necessary in the business world primarily because it makes a company more competitive. As a premise, **a company that has a servant leader in a critical role is one that is going to inextricably link the needs of both the business and its people**. This competitive advantage is difficult to duplicate because it involves fitting the accurate personality to serve as a teacher, encourager, and helper for others to reach their potential. Since servant leaders are responsible for caring for and nurturing individuals who may require emotional, professional, and social guidance, the role may be unideal for most. Undoubtedly, **a true servant leader is called to serve with certain talents and skills given by God at birth, with other competencies further developed through personal and professional development.**

Christian leaders are servant leaders in secular environments. This spiritual type of servant leadership, one that admonishes godly principles, is needed in today's competitive business environment. Many situations and circumstances could be avoided when and if Christian principles are used in business engagement. Spiritual leaders can be the most trustworthy and loyal people to work for. In this context, great leadership can focus on the potential of others, esteeming and supplying them with the tools to accelerate their goals and aspirations, which ultimately allows an organization to utilize people with God-given skills to accomplish great things. As determined by most practitioners, good leadership should consist of the physical and emotional support needed to enable people to perform their job functions to the best of their abilities. Both competencies, physical and emotional, acknowledge that people are fulfilled in a variety of ways. What motivates one may not motivate another.

SERVANT LEADERSHIP IN THE BIBLE

There are many examples in the Bible that address the strategic objective of leading as a servant leader using godly principles. In both the Old and New Testaments, learners will find a commonality in the word of God where leadership is defined differently than exacerbated today. In the New Testament, Barnabas was known as one example of a Biblical leader who could bridge the gaps of differing opinions. Masterfully, he could envision what was and what could be. He was referred to as the "son of encouragement" (Acts 4:36). Notably, he bridged the gaps by serving both the Greek and Jewish worlds in the times of the early churches. By doing this, Barnabas was able to be a compassionate Christian leader well-trusted by other leaders like Paul. In a stark example of leading by foreseeing a better future, Barnabas fittingly defended John Mark from Paul's aggressive behavior. Barnabas saw the potential in John Mark and withstood Paul's disapproval of him. In the end, Barnabas's foresight into John Mark's future value would come to fruition as he would come to spend time with Paul during his last imprisonment and provide valuable support to Peter. As demonstrated by Barnabas, leadership encompasses the ability to serve others when it is not popular to do so.

From the Old Testament, useful servant leadership tactics can be gleaned from important leaders of that time. One such example can be found in the book of Jeremiah. Leaders can learn from Jeremiah's response to his servant Baruch, who appeared to be enamored with an opportunity to gain a place in stardom. In Jeremiah 45:5 (KJV), Jeremiah said, "Should you then seek great things for yourself? Seek them not." In other words, Jeremiah aimed to save his wayward-thinking servant by prophesying a truth about stardom and where it leads. As a Christian, it is understood that "great things" would be accomplished by serving the Lord. 1 Timothy 3:1 (NLT) says that aspiring to leadership is an honorable thing. However, the admonishment that any of these accomplishments would be "for yourself" would end in inevitable disappointment.

Jesus did not live a rich and famous life but remained ambitious about serving others to do God's will. His intent was never self-seeking. **Servant leaders should recognize that they are first and foremost a steward in whom his work would be quite the opposite of one who simply desires to accomplish a thing for themselves.** He should not be self-serving, looking for a result that increases his finances or work that improves his reputation. In Philippians 2:7 (ESV), Paul tells us that Jesus "made himself of no reputation." Jesus did not want any of the glory to come to himself for all the many works that he would do during his ministry. Jesus designated his life to be of no concern with prestige, promotion, value, or commodity. The servant leader should be of the same foundation.

In the example of Joseph in the book of Genesis, learners can see that he became a servant leader because of the rejection he suffered early in life. In the Old Testament, the story of Joseph is most notable because of the leader he became despite the abandonment in his life. The abandonment Joseph suffered was at the hands of his family. His older brothers, who he understandably looked up to, conspired against him. Ultimately, he was sold by the people who loved him.

Nevertheless, Joseph endured rejection and exemplified great strength in the face of immense pain. Genesis 45 (NLT) explains Joseph's long-awaited travail but eventual forgiveness of his faint-hearted brothers who sold him as a slave approximately 15 years prior (Gen 41 KJV). This was an opportunity for Joseph, who had become the Overseer to the King of Egypt, to take vengeance on his seemingly cowardly brothers. However, Joseph identified the area of sin before he allowed it to take hold of him. Instead, he became a servant to his family once again. Understanding his true purpose and reason for being in the position he held, Joseph said: "God sent me ahead of you to save life and preserve our family" (Gen 45:5 AMP).

SERVANT LEADERSHIP STYLE

Of the multiple New Testament servant leaders, an examination of the life of Paul and the object of pride that he avoided garnered him apostleship in the Gospel of Jesus Christ. Indeed, Paul was the most successful missionary and leader of the New Testament church. However, his life remained imperiled by the risk of assailing himself higher than Jesus Christ. With careful intentions, Paul made comprehensive attempts to ensure his focus was on serving those who needed the Gospel and not on building his own name. In I Corinthians 9:27 NIV, Paul proclaims a fear of being disqualified if ever found to be with pride. Relating to the training of an athlete, Paul pronounces a regimen of discipline that begins with the flesh. According to Paul, it is the body that is at war with God and the spiritual nature of Jesus Christ (Rom 7:22 NIV). Even so, leaders should be reminded that the "struggle is not against flesh and blood, but against the rulers, against the authorities, against the powers of this dark world and against the spiritual forces of evil in the heavenly realms" (Eph 6:12 NIV).

As a servant leader who directed the rebuilding of Jerusalem's walls after the Babylonian exile, Nehemiah's leadership bar was high. His accomplishments were phenomenal for the time in which he lived. However, Oswald

J. Sanders (2006) concluded that the Apostle Peter is perhaps the character that most closely aligns with the day-to-day struggle of the Christian leader. Contrastingly, Christians can gain a more comprehensive view of Peter at his worst and best. As he denied knowing Jesus three times, we see the very worst of Peter in endurance, character, and integrity (John 18:15-27 KJV). Invariably, we recall the command of Jesus to Peter saying, "Feed my sheep" (John 21:15 KJV). After recounting his failure in denying his relationship with Christ three times, Peter would become the patriarch upon which the early church was built, with special instructions as the mediator of the Gospel to the Jews. Initially, Peter was self-centered; then, he became others-centered, focusing on serving those he led.

PROJECT MANAGER AND SERVANTHOOD

As a learnable behavior, servant leadership can be a formidable skill set for a project manager to obtain. Effectively, project managers need other people to complete their assigned tasks to succeed. The activities of a project manager seldom include the completion of deliverables that are owned by himself. In fact, a project manager is commonly referred to as a scheduler or coordinator of people. To this end, they direct the execution of tasks and activities of others rather than directly performing them themselves. In his 2013 book called *The Synergist "How to Lead Your Team to Predictable Success"*, Les McKeown describes the project management role as a "synergist". **The project manager is a member of the team, but he or she is perhaps the most vital in the role of uniting the team together. As a synergist, the project manager bridges the divide between related activities to build continuity within the team.** This is ultimately needed to corrugate the team around a central purpose and goal towards success. Since projects are inherently temporary, synergy is required early in the phase of team development and quickly to ensure difficult challenges can be resolved adequately. In Tuckman's Ladder of forming, storming, norming and performing, project teams have a short rung. Therefore, project managers must excel at expeditiously getting the team into a productive stride. For the project team, the stages of development are much more imperative to accomplish before resources are released for the next assignment. Tuckman's Ladder depicts this challenge and constructs a tangible illustration of what an effective project manager should expect. (See figure 3)

Figure 3: Tuckman's Team Development Ladder taken from pmstudycircle.com.

Stage	Key Elements
Forming	• Orientation of task and team • Ground rules identified for team • Dependent on the leader
Storming	• Team members start getting to know each other and understand their roles and responsibilities • Uncertainty, anxiety, and resistance from the team • Conflict and crisis among the team
Norming	• Team members have a sound understanding of their roles and responsibilities, and they begin to work together and adjust their habits and behavior • Information exchanged, emotional support among team members and cohesion
Performing	• Team members are acting like one, interdependent and adjusted • Team can start working with less supervision. • Sustainment of task achieved
Adjourning	• The project is completed • The project team disbands

As a servant leader, a project manager's care is placed and focused on otherness. Servant leadership calls for the goals of each team member to be extracted into the project's goals. One goal of the project manager is to encourage team members to achieve individual success so that everyone can share in achievements. Servant leaders have characteristics of being supportive, compassionate, empathetic, sympathetic, attentive, and effective at relationship building. As part of a caring leadership style, serving others is a dominating distinction for servanthood. It is not uncommon for a leader practicing servanthood to expend most effort improving the environment for others while sacrificing desires for self-fulfillment. This quality of selflessness is a required attribute all leaders should have. **Leaders who are good stewards of resources are particularly aware of their most valuable commodity – people.** Without the contribution and buy-in of team members, a leader cannot succeed, especially for a highly effective project manager. People who are served by their leaders feel valued and included as an essential part of the team. While it is important to ensure that the leader's vision is clearly understood and carried out, a servant leader involves the aspirations and desires of others in an attempt to meet the needs of all.

The negative connotations regarding servanthood are obvious and somewhat similar to that of being a follower. Many leaders perceive servanthood, to any great extent, to be a weakness in authority and subversion of power. Servanthood can counter a leader who desires to be perceived as powerful and in command of his or her vision. Diverting to the needs and desires of others may appear to the leader as being out of control. Leaders who tend to admonish approaches within the *commanding leadership style* will have the strongest defiance to aligning themselves to the selfless attributes of servanthood. Even though the characteristics of a commanding leadership style may be required to propel project teams past impossible goals, the approach should be reserved for strategic and situational purposes only. If employed for an extensive length of time, a command leadership style results in disgruntled team members' attrition.

A servant leader's common characteristics are comparable to those of a highly effective project manager whose attributes are widely seen as impactful to the team. Based on principles, Christian leaders are purported to be most closely aligned with the qualities of a servant. An easy comparison of Christian leaders from the Bible lends unmistakably to skillful men of God who put others first. Abraham, Moses, Joshua, and Paul are prime examples of servant leadership whereby the well-being of their people was most important. Regardless of their people's needs, these leaders sought God's answers. In each story about leaders in the Bible, one will find the overarching theme of care, compassion, and support towards people. As noted, Jesus Christ was the most notable leader in the Bible. He illustrated selflessness without any concern for his own well-being. Jesus understood his role as the ideal servant leader and how his example would be a model for aspiring leaders for years to come. **Project managers aspiring to be servant leaders can learn from the exhibit of Christian principles. Though a servant leader may not purport to be a Christian, his principles can be highly moral and Christ-like.**

10 TRANSFORMATIONAL LEADERSHIP STYLE

Robert Greenleaf (1970), perhaps the most influential thinker on leadership approaches, frames the context of leading in terms of successfully gaining or losing followers. In the case of the project team, we would translate the term "followers" into "team members." Leadership theorist James C. Burns (1978) would later liken popular leadership approaches to the Roman Empire era, where there was a King or Prophet who ruled over the kingdom. In ancient times, leadership was assumed by inheritance or birthright. Today, effective leadership is earned by masterful inspiration.

The buzzword for inspirational leadership is "transformational." *Transformational leadership* sounds better when talking about it, looks better as a credential on a social media profile, and makes people feel better when they claim to use it. Regardless of popular tendencies, transformational leadership has proven to be more effective than its chief competitor, *transactional leadership*. As one of the most popular and well-known leadership approaches in the 21st century, the transformational approach has become synonymous with best-in-class practice (Bass & Riggio, 2006). With origins from the "great man" theory, transformational leadership can alter an entire group's culture, attitude, and goals. **Effectively, transformational leaders can connect to team members on a common level where emotions can be linked together. As a result, they become loyal and devoted to a trustworthy ideal encapsulated in the common ideas of the team.**

Applicable to the study of transformational components of leadership, Isaac Boateng (2014) measured several characteristics, including influence, motivation, stimulation, and consideration. His leadership study used a questionnaire to measure the degree of each characteristic found in each leader. The results of the surveyed leaders concluded that the strongest transformational leadership characteristic was the ability to motivate others, while the weakest was the ability to consider others. Transformational leaders who address difficult environments with a charismatic approach often rely on natural skills. Such skills are difficult to duplicate or mimic in real-world practice. Moreover, it isn't easy to develop an education or training program in which aspiring leaders can grasp transformational leadership's primary concepts and theories.

Famous leaders in world history have exhibited a natural behavior relative to their beliefs. President Abraham Lincoln strongly believed that slavery was wrong. He was instrumental in urging congressional leaders to agree to the tenets of the 13th Amendment to the U.S. Constitution, which ultimately abolished slavery. Another example can be found in the service of Prime Minister Winston Churchill. His values compelled him to stand strong while Nazi Germany attacked British shores. He led an active resistance of "no-compromise" against Adolf Hitler that ultimately resulted in Nazi Germany's defeat. In opposite parts of the world, Lincoln and Churchill established personal beliefs shared by their constituents. By establishing common purposes, both men were able to react positively to the challenges of their time and lead transformational changes in world history.

TRANSFORMATIONAL LEADERSHIP STYLE

Another example of transformational leadership can be seen in the first Black South African president, Nelson Mandela. Mandela was an inspirational figure who engaged allies and critics alike with his charisma. Seen as an emotional component of leadership (Antonakis, 2012), charisma intricately links traits and transformational leadership. The charisma factor in transformational leadership is often recognized as a popular trait in the person that many people would like to be. Mandela was viewed by his followers as a selfless leader of great trustworthiness. As a leader sentenced to prison due to the apartheid struggle in South Africa, Mandela returned to the people of South Africa with the intention of governing them into peace. His dynamic qualities and ability to communicate transformed an entire nation.

Adolf Hitler is an example of a transformational leader who led the German people with the persona known as the "great man" (Jung & Sosik, 2006). His constituents believed that a pure generation of German people would create an incubation for the next generations' supreme intellect and physiology. To accomplish Hitler's ideals, the mass incarceration and genocide of Jews were steps on the path of one of the greatest evils of all time. Amongst the vilest dictators and world leaders, Hitler amassed a following of willing co-conspirators. Defeat was inevitable as dominant world leaders defended their countries from Hitler's dastardly aggression. Among the fearless respondents, Prime Minister Winston Churchill of England led a global retort that thwarted Hitler's powerful force. The factors of charisma attached emotions of grandeur to Hitler's agenda. With the use of Emotional Intelligence (EI) and shared opulence of supremacy, Hitler represented an amassed people deprived of external realities, focusing on compelling rhetoric of purity and exceptionalism. According to German prognosticators, Hitler was the "great man" that theorists referred to, whereby followers became inextricably linked through shared ambition and motivations (Kouzes & Posner, 2007). As a result, history has proved that a transformational leadership style can be used for good or evil.

Transformation Leadership and Project Managers. To unify the project team, where members are only temporarily assigned with different backgrounds in belief, culture, ethnicity and values, a project manager should start by figuring out how the project goals can be common among all the team members. The team must share some common

TRANSFORMATIONAL LEADERSHIP STYLE

beliefs about the goals that can be leveraged to unify the team's effort. One of the qualities of a highly effective project manager that must stand out to the team is a strong belief in a set of principles. This quality in a transformative leader can penetrate the personal motivations and aspirations of team members and join them together. As a result, the project team can buy into the cohesive relationship created when common goals are shared between individuals. Such a relationship can cause team members to be extremely loyal and self-giving towards one another and the project's goals.

PART III
AN EMPIRICAL STUDY OF LEADERSHIP

11 AN INDUCTIVE LOOK INTO LEADERSHIP

In 2019, I completed research for my PhD dissertation that looked at what style or approach to leadership creates a successful outcome on a project management team; specifically, the research question asked: What is the relationship, if any, between successful technology project outcomes and project managers who practice a servant style of leadership? My study investigated the success of technology projects based on a recommendation drawn from a 2010 study published by Kenneth N. Thompson, who evaluated successful projects and servant leadership across multiple industries. Thompson suggested that future studies engage in more exclusive research into specific sectors to identify new correlations to be added to the body of academic knowledge on this subject. The context of examining successful technology projects and characteristics of servant leadership in my study was based on three critical background factors:

1. Two out of three corporate initiatives assigned as "technology projects" failed due to extenuating circumstances (Nelson, 2014). Reasons for failure range from bad requirements, cost overspend, schedule overrun or ineffective leadership.
2. Leadership starts with the assigned project manager. Project managers must lead their teams (followers) with specific tools, techniques, and methods in order to be effective (Binder, 2007). The benefit of employing a project management professional is an exponential increase in the effective management of expectations and risks (Kendrick, 2015).
3. The servant leadership style has emerged in the 21st century as a credible approach in a business. Servant leadership has become a popular theory and has proceeded to tap into an entirely new source of human motivation (Greenleaf, 1977).

DISCUSSION OF THE STUDY

Similar to Thompson's (2010) research, my study used theoretical literature encompassing several experts who have solidified the primary assumptions pertaining to leadership styles and project management (Alleman, 2014; Arora & Baronikian, 2013; Perry, 2011; Sparrow, 2017; Wills, 2015). Each ascertained the dilemma plaguing most projects — the majority of them result in failing outcomes. Earlier dated literature research into leadership styles and characteristics did not present any evidence of an increase in successful project outcomes (Berg & Karlsen, 2007; Cheng & Moore, 2005; Dainty, Gehring, 2007; Hauschildt, Gesche, & Medcof, 2000; Hyvari, 2006; Kezsbom, 1998; Kodjababian & Petty, 2007; Neuhauser, 2007; Schmid & Adams, 2008; Thoms & Pinto, 1999; Turner & Muller, 2005). More recent empirical studies have shown some reliable correlations between certain leadership styles and successful project outcomes (Alleman, 2014; Arora & Baronikian, 2013; Perry, 2011; Sparrow, 2017; Thompson, 2010; Wills, 2015). However, the most recent reporting of industry project outcomes remains at an unacceptable rate of failure. My observations were captured from respondents' answers drawn from the online survey data. Survey respondents were members of the Project Management Institute (PMI) who were associated with individual chapters located across the United States and U.S. Territories.

There were 49 respondents who answered all 14 close-ended and three Likert scale questions completely. Respondents answered questions pertaining to the ten independent variables of active listening, empathy, healing, awareness, persuasion, conceptualization, foresight, stewardship, commitment to growth, and community building derived from Spears (2002). These independent variables were successfully examined and cross-tabulated against six project success factors whereby each respondent agreed or strongly agreed were viable. The six factors were derived from PMI's reference to attributes of successful project outcomes (2008): Effective scope management, adherence to project schedule and budget, meeting project requirements, stakeholder objectives, and user performance needs. Findings calculated in the Statistical Product and Service Solutions tool (SPSS) demonstrated that the instrument used in collecting respondents' answers was accurate, consistent, and reliable. Tests of each hypothesis revealed findings showing a probability and predictability of occurrences in servant leadership and successful project outcome answers. The tests found a strong existence of significant differences between observed and expected data for each servant leadership attribute, thereby determining a rejection of each null hypothesis.

Analysis revealed the existence of a relationship between all ten servant leadership attributes and successful project outcome responses. However, linear calculations for the servant leadership attribute of forward-thinking exposed an insignificant relationship with successful project outcomes. The forward-thinking linear results found that the relationship was negative toward strength, indicating an inconsistent association with respondents' answers. Although the symmetric tests performed on forward-thinking and successful technology project outcomes showed a moderate strength indication of a relationship, signifying that a relationship exists, regression and other cross-tabulation decanted a significant relationship.

IMPLICATIONS OF THE STUDY

The implications of this study led me to ascertain that

project managers exhibiting or striving to exhibit servant leadership characteristics can increase their potential to manage successful projects. Although the results did not show any significant correlation, a correlation exists. Of the many leadership styles that drive performance and success on a team, this study can lead readers to conclude that servant leadership skills are viable for aspiring project managers to consider when determining applicable training options. Organizations looking at this study should distinguish between leadership styles with empirical evidence supporting correlation with success and those without evidence.

LEADERSHIP TRAINING

Since leadership training is widely expected and provided in most organizations today, there is a higher onus on companies to select content that is relevant and proven effective in delivering results for their employees. Most survey respondents participated in formal leadership training (see Table 3). Only 12.2% reported that they had not received any formal leadership training. The implication drawn from the high frequency of project managers formally trained in leadership led me to ascertain that the responses in the survey reflect individuals who have been exposed to best practices and standards in leadership.

Table 3: Received Formal Leadership Training

Formal Training	Frequency	Percent	Valid Percent	Cumulative Percent
Yes	43	87.8	87.8	87.8
No	6	12.2	12.2	100.0
Total	49	100.0	100.0	

DOMINATE LEADERSHIP STYLES

Based on their experience, respondents believed that project managers' most dominant leadership style was involving others in decision-making, striving for unity, listening, and explaining (see Table 4). A high of 40.8% of project managers involved others, while a low of 4.1% used charisma and values as a dominant leadership style with their project teams. The implication is that project managers are currently employing characteristics of servant leadership such as effective listening, growing community, and healing relationships as a dominating tactic in managing projects. This study empirically proved these characteristics to correlate with successful project outcomes. The low number implies that less dominant servant leadership styles are not being applied by project managers, such as using intuition in facing situations or foresight to address issues, both of which did not show empirical evidence of a strong correlation to successful project outcomes in my study.

Table 4: Leadership Styles Most Dominant in Project Managers

Styles	Frequency	Percent	Valid Percent	Cumulative Percent
Charismatic, creative, empowering, inspirational, visionary	2	4.1	4.1	4.1
Clarifies subordinate roles and task requirements in return for rewards	5	10.2	10.2	14.3
Makes decisions based on the situation	10	20.4	20.4	34.7
Role model, is accountable, sets high standards and expectations	6	12.2	12.2	46.9
Establishes vision and sets direction	4	8.2	8.2	55.1
Affirms and articulates values, represents the organization	2	4.1	4.1	59.2
Involves others in decision making, strives for unity, listens and explains	20	40.8	40.8	100.0
Total	49	100.0	100.0	

BEST RESULTS LEADERSHIP STYLE

Based on their experience, respondents believed that the leadership style that achieved the best results for project managers included involving others in decision-making, striving for unity, listening, and explaining (see Table 5). A high of 40.8% of project managers involved others in obtaining the best outcome, while a low of 2% used the affirmation of values as a leadership style to gain the best results with their project teams. Employing a leadership style with characteristics such as charisma, creativity, and empowerment was less dominantly used by project managers at 4.1% (see Table 4); however, 12.2% of respondents reported that project managers had better results when they applied these tactics (see Table 5). The implication is that project managers are achieving the best results from characteristics of servant leadership, such as serving others, growing people and healing relationships, which are also dominant tactics for managing projects. These characteristics were empirically proven in this study to correlate with successful project outcomes. The low number of 2% implies that the best results are not being gained when project managers use tactics that involve affirming and articulating values with their project team.

Table 5: Leadership Styles (attributes) that Achieved Best Results for Project Managers

Styles	Frequency	Percent	Valid Percent	Cumulative Percent
Charismatic, creative, empowering, inspirational, visionary	6	12.2	12.2	12.2
Clarifies subordinate roles and task requirements in return for rewards	3	6.1	6.1	18.4
Role model, is accountable, sets high standards and expectations	11	22.4	22.4	40.8
Establishes vision and sets direction	8	16.3	16.3	57.1
Affirms and articulates values, represents the organization	1	2.0	2.0	59.2
Involves others in decision making, strives for unity, listens and explains	20	40.8	40.8	100.0
Total	49	100.0	100.0	

EFFECTIVE PROJECT MANAGERS

Using a list of 19 characteristics of an effective leader, survey respondents were asked to rate the degree to which they agreed or disagreed that each characteristic was effective on a seven-point Likert scale. The scale ranged

AN INDUCTIVE LOOK INTO LEADERSHIP

from one, which was strongly agreed, to seven, which was strongly disagreed. The minimum value of one assigned to each of the 19 leadership characteristics indicates at least one respondent strongly agreed that all 19 leadership characteristics were effective (see Table 6). Of all the responses, being "technically competent" was the only leadership characteristic a respondent disagreed with was effective for a project manager.

The lowest mean for all effective leadership characteristics was 1.22, representing the leadership characteristic of communicating well, implying strong agreement across all respondents with a standard deviation of .42. Other leadership characteristics that respondents agreed with less strongly were indicated by higher means. Being a visionary, creating and sharing identity, managing corporate culture, and being technically competent represented the highest means, ranging from 2.32 to 2.71, with variations ranging from .891 to 1.79, which was still within the *agree to slightly agree* responses. The implication is that all 19 leadership characteristics are effective skills for existing or aspiring project managers to obtain, with small to negligible differences inferred from the data.

Table 6: Effective Leadership Characteristics for Project Managers

Characteristics	N	Range	Minimum	Maximum	Sum	Mean	Std. Deviation	Variance
Ability to motivate	49	2.00	1.00	3.00	76.00	1.5510	.61445	.378
Adaptable to change	49	2.00	1.00	3.00	69.00	1.4082	.57440	.330
Being a visionary	49	4.00	1.00	5.00	114.00	2.3265	1.02851	1.058
Being decisive	49	2.00	1.00	3.00	81.00	1.6531	.59690	.356
Building relationships	49	4.00	1.00	5.00	67.00	1.3673	.69803	.487
Conflict resolution	49	2.00	1.00	3.00	81.00	1.6531	.63084	.398
Create a shared identity	49	3.00	1.00	4.00	114.00	2.3265	.94401	.891
Displays credibility	49	3.00	1.00	4.00	77.00	1.5714	.81650	.667
Emotional maturity	49	4.00	1.00	5.00	78.00	1.5918	.91101	.830
Good communicator	49	1.00	1.00	2.00	60.00	1.2245	.42157	.178
Guides and energizes team	49	2.00	1.00	3.00	87.00	1.7755	.71488	.511
Inspire project team	49	3.00	1.00	4.00	94.00	1.9184	.73134	.535
Leading by example	49	3.00	1.00	4.00	75.00	1.5306	.71011	.504
Manage corporate culture	49	4.00	1.00	5.00	115.00	2.3469	1.01141	1.023
Manage stress	49	4.00	1.00	5.00	97.00	1.9796	1.01015	1.020
Promote team work	49	3.00	1.00	4.00	85.00	1.7347	.78463	.616
Remove obstacles to progress	49	4.00	1.00	5.00	72.00	1.4694	.73886	.546
Strong sense of commitment	49	3.00	1.00	4.00	79.00	1.6122	.67133	.451
Technically competent	49	5.00	1.00	6.00	133.00	2.7143	1.33853	1.792
Valid N (listwise)	49							

12 FINAL THOUGHTS AND CONCLUSIONS

Leadership is an ongoing journey of self-discovery, growth, and improvement. It involves a commitment to personal development, a willingness to embrace challenges within oneself, and the ability to inspire and motivate oneself toward achieving meaningful goals. Much of the leader's development happens with their personal approach to life. It has as much to do with where you spend your time as with where you do not spend your time. The Bible declares that *out of the abundance of a person's heart is how he or she will speak*. So, habits, routines and time spent considerably impact the outcome of who and what a person becomes. I have spent a significant amount of time in research, study and observation, extolling to experiment and apply best practices that I have learned. My personal, professional, and empirical learnings have been immensely beneficial. Here are seven commitments I will leave you with that I have discovered while on my leadership journey that have assisted and abetted me in becoming a valuable team member and effective leader.

7 Commitments to Highly Effective Leadership

1. Commit to Self-Awareness:
- Spend the majority of your time improving on your strengths and what you do well.
- Don't spend significant effort addressing weaknesses especially if you can delegate something you do not do well to someone else.
- Inwardly reflect on your thoughts and behaviors to gain insights into your actions and how they impact others. Make adjustments to gain positive and favorable reactions from others.

2. Commit to being Proactive:
- Take the initiative to identify and pursue opportunities that meet your personal requirements and not just the requirements of others.
- Break down larger goals into smaller, achievable tasks and incrementally accomplish the small goals one by one.

FINAL THOUGHTS AND CONCLUSIONS

- Demonstrate a willingness to go above and beyond basic expectations; however always under promise and over deliver.

3. Commit to being Accountable:

- Prioritize tasks and activities based on importance, urgency, and severity. Problems (issues) should be fixed as soon as possible; a risk should have a remediation plan to prevent future negative impacts.
- Set realistic, achievable deadlines and manage your time based on your capacity. This is the definition of accountability.
- Avoid procrastination and stay focused on completing high-priority tasks on time while positioning lower priority items on a backlog.

4. Commit to being Responsible:

- The buck stops with you as a leader. Accept the fact that your head will roll if something goes wrong. Loyal team members will be cognizant of your dilemma and work very hard to be accountable.
- Solve problems today. A problem is an impediment that is causing a delay, overrun or rework; therefore, it must be solved expeditiously so that the team is no longer negatively impacted.

- Communicate clearly and openly with the goal of answering all answerable questions. Listen actively and attentively to affirmatively understand other's viewpoints.

5. Commit to an Agile Mindset:
- Embrace changes based on new unplanned priorities and reprioritize appropriately.
- Fail fast and learn from mistakes. Always seek feedback and incorporate it into the next event, task, or activity. View failure as an opportunity for growth.
- Maintain a positive attitude and make things easy for others, not hard. An easy-going mindset is a personal favorite of mine – the old adages that say "pain equals gain" and "adversity equals progress" are dead!

6. Commit to Continuously Learning:
- Cultivate a growth mindset and a willingness to learn as a way of life.
- Remain plugged in and informed about the latest trends in your industry and domain.
- Look for tools, techniques and best practices that improve your way of working and the lives of others.

7. Commit to Building Relationships:
- Build a strong professional network through relationships with colleagues, friends, and acquaintances.
- Foster positive relationships with colleagues, mentors, and others in your industry.
- Reach out periodically to others to recognize them when they have a special day, a promotion or after a recent interaction.

CONCLUSION

To form the inextricable link required to orchestrate trust, faith, and loyalty in a leader, a masterful inspiration must be created with their team. If intangible qualities are not used, then leadership is typically derived from inheritance, position, or tenure. Most leaders have appointed positions which establish their leadership authority. **Most of the people I know who have become highly effective leaders have developed intangible qualities that have earned respect from their team. However, truly inspirational leaders are few, far and in between, but not impossible to mimic, match or exceed.** The seven commitments can be used to enhance your leadership effectiveness (See Appendix - Dale Leadership Effectiveness Matrix).

FINAL THOUGHTS AND CONCLUSIONS

One of the goals of all research, with a qualitative or quantitative lens, is to advance the subject matter utilizing evidence that proves or disproves a theory or idea. Through an exhaustive study of a subject's various components and factors, data is used to draw measurable conclusions with degrees of certainty, given the evaluation of the variables examined. Project management and effective leadership have been my subjects of study for the last 20 years. I continue on a journey to observe and evaluate the effectiveness of one leadership style over the other. Depending on the industry, environment, and team type, one leadership style can be more effective than another, as illustrated in this book. We, the researchers and practitioners, understand that no fixed leadership style can be effective across all industries and domains. However, I aspire that the theoretical reflection and empirical evidence provided in this book will guide applicable leadership approaches. It is my highest hope that my personal, professional, and inductive journey into best practices and effectiveness in leadership will lead existing and ambitious project professionals to grasp for the stars while utilizing the vast amount of evidence and proven ways of working to support their work.

REFERENCES

Alleman, G. B. (2014). Performance-Based Project Management: Increasing the Probability of Project Success. New York, NY: AMACOM.

Antonakis, J. (2012). *Transformational and charismatic leadership*. In D. V. Day & J.

Antonakis (Eds.), *The nature of leadership* (2nd ed., pp. 256– 288). Thousand Oaks, CA: Sage.

Arora, M. & Baronikian, H. (2013). Leadership in Project Management. Leading People and

Projects to Success 2nd ed. Leadership Publishing.

Bass, B. M., & Avolio, B. J. (1990). The implications of transactional and transformational leadership for individual, team, and organizational development. Research in Organizational Change and Development, 4, 231-272.

REFERENCES

Bass, B. M., & Avolio, B. J. (1997). Full Range Leadership Development: Manual for the Multifactor Leadership Questionnaire. Palo Alto, CA. Mind Garden.

Bass, B. & Riggio, R. (2006). *Transformational leadership.* New York, NY: Psychology Press.

Beldoch, M. (1964), *Sensitivity to expression of emotional meaning in three modes of communication,* in J. R. Davitz et al., The Communication of Emotional Meaning, McGraw-Hill, pp. 31-42.

Berg, M. E., & Karlsen, J. T. (2007). Mental models in project management coaching. *Engineering Management Journal, 19*(3), 3-14.

Binder, J. (2007). *Global Project Management: Communication, Collaboration and Management Across Borders*: Gower.

Blanchard, K. (2003). *Servant Leader.* Nashville, TN: Thomas Nelson.

Blanchard, K., Zigarmi, P. & Zigarmi, D. (1985). *Leadership and the One Minute Manager.*

Scranton, PA: William Morrow & Co. Blake, R. R. & Mouton, J. S. (1964). *The Managerial Grid: The Key to Leadership Excellence.*

Houston: Gulf Publishing Co. Boateng, I. (2014). *A quantitative case study of transformational leadership characteristics of valley view university in Ghana*

REFERENCES

(Order No. 3630814). Available from ProQuest Dissertations & Theses Global. (1564230118). Retrieved from https://search.proquest.com/docview/1564230118?accountid=165104.

Burns, J. M. (1978). *Leadership.* New York, NY: Harper Torchbooks.

Dainty, A., Cheng, M., & Moore, D. (2005). Competency-based model for predicting construction project managers' performance. *Journal of Management in Engineering, 21*(1), 2-9.

Davitz, J. R. 1964. *The communication of emotional meaning.* New York: McGraw-Hill.

Fiedler, F. E. & Garcia, J. E. (1987). *New approaches to leadership: Cognitive resources and organizational performance.* New York: Wiley.

Fiorina, C. (2007). *Tough Choices: A Memoir.* Colorado Springs, CO: Penguin.

Flint, B. (2012). *The journey to competitive advantage through servant leadership.* Indiana: WestBow Press.

Giuliani, R. W. (2002). *Leadership.* (1st ed.). New York, N.Y.: Miramax books.

Goleman, D. (1995). *Why It Can Matter More Than IQ.* New York, NY: Bantam.

REFERENCES

Goleman, D., Boyatiz, R.E., & McKee, A. (2004). *Primal leadership: Learning to Lead With.*

Greenleaf, R. K. (1970). *The servant as leader.* Newton Centre, MA: Robert K. Greenleaf.

Greenleaf, R. K. (1977). *Servant Leadership: A Journey into the Nature of Legitimate Power and Greatness.* Mahwah, NJ: Paulist Press.

Hauschildt, J., Gesche, K., & Medcof, J. (2000). Realistic criteria for project managers. *Selection and Development, 31*(3), 23-32.

Hersey, P. (1985). *The Situational Leader.* New York, NY: Warner Books.

Hersey, P., & Blanchard, K. H. (1988). *Management of organizational behavior: Utilizing human resources.* Englewood Cliffs, NJ: Prentice Hall.

House, R. J., & Mitchell, R. R. (1974). *Path-goal theory of leadership.* Journal of Contemporary Business, 3, 81-97.

Hyvari, I. (2006). Success of projects in different organizational conditions. *Project Management Journal, 37*(4), 31-41.

Janis, R. S. (2003). *An examination of bass's (1985) leadership theory in the project management environment* (Order No. 3108623), (305236420).

REFERENCES

Retrieved from https://search.proquest.com/docview/305236420?accountid=39317.

Jordan, M. & Vancil, M. (1994). *I Can't Accept Not Trying: Michael Jordan on the Pursuit of Excellence*. San Francisco, CA: Harper.

Juneja, P. (2013). *The Management Study Guide*. Retrieved from https://managementstudyguide.com/blake-mouton-managerial-grid.htm on May 6, 2017.

Jung, D., & Sosik, J. J. (2006). *Who are the spellbinders? Identifying personal attributes of charismatic leaders*. Journal of Leadership & Organizational Studies, 12, 12–27.

Kendrick, T. (2015). *Identifying and Managing Project Risk: Essential Tools for Failure-Proofing Your Project (3rd ed.)*: AMACON.

Kezsbom, D. S. (1988). Leadership and influence: The challenge of project management. *American Association of Cost Engineers, 1*(2), 121-126.

Kodjababian, J., & Petty, J. (2007). Dedicated project leadership: Helping organizations meet strategic goals. *Healthcare Financial Management, 61*(11), 130-135.

Kouzes, J. M., & Posner, B. Z. (2007). *The leadership challenge* (3rd ed.). San Francisco: Jossey-Bass.

Lencioni, P. (2002). *The Five Dysfunctions of a Team*. San Francisco: Jossey-Bass.

REFERENCES

Lee, M. R. (2010). *E-leadership for project managers: A study of situational leadership and virtual project success* (Order No. 3409339). Available from ProQuest Dissertations & Theses Global. (717581516). Retrieved from https://search.proquest.com/docview/717581516?accountid=165104.

Likert, R. (1967). The Human Organization: Its Management and Value. New York, NY: Mcgraw-Hill.

Little, S. D. (2010). *Perception or reality? A frame analysis of leadership behavior, style, and effectiveness among selected community college administrators* (Order No. 3439268). Available from ProQuest Dissertations & Theses Global. (851182776). Retrieved from http://search.proquest.com/docview/851182776?accountid=165104.

Mayer, J. D. (2004). Emotional Intelligence: Key Readings on the Mayer and Salovey Model.

Naples, FL: National Professional Resources, Inc./Dude Publishing.

Mayer, J.D., Salovey, P., Caruso, D.R. (2002). *Mayer-Salovey-Caruso Emotional Intelligence*

Test (MSCEIT) User's Manual. Toronto, Canada: MHS Publishers.

REFERENCES

McCaffery, P. (2004). *The Higher Education Manager's Handbook*. New York, NY: Routledge.

Mes, C. J. (1983). *Principle Leadership Style and Its Relationship to Teach*

Job Satisfaction as Moderated by Selected Contingency Factors (Order No. 8401630). Available from ProQuest Dissertations & Theses Global. (303191697). Retrieved from http://search.proquest.com/docview/303191697?accountid=165104.

Nelson, R. R. (2014). *IT Project Management: Infamous Failures, Classic Mistakes, and Best Practices*: Amazon Digital Services, Inc.

Neuhauser, C. (2007). Project manager leadership behaviors and frequency of use by female project managers. *Project Management Journal, 38*(1), 21-31.

Northouse, P. G. (2007). *Introduction to Leadership: Concepts & Practice*. Thousand Oaks, CA: SAGE Publications.

Payne, W.L. (1983). A study of emotion: developing emotional intelligence. *Dissertation*

Abstracts International 47, p. 203A (University microfilms No. AAC 8605928).

Perry, M. P. (2011). *Business Driven Project Portfolio Management: Conquering the 10 risks that threaten success*. Fort Lauderdale, FL: J. Ross Publishing.

REFERENCES

Project Management Institute (2021). *Earning Power: Project Management Salary Survey, Ninth Edition*. Newtown Square, PA: PMI Publications.

Riggio, R. & Bass, B. (1997). *Transformational Leadership: Industrial, Military, and Educational Impact*. New York, NY: Psychology Press.

Rodin, S. (2010). *The Steward Leader: Transforming people, organizations and communities,* Downers Grove, Ill: IVP Academic.

Sanders, Oswald J. (2006). *Spiritual Leadership: Principles of Excellence for Every Believer*. Moody Publishers.

Situational Leadership Model (1960). Retrieved from file:///C:/Users/md7603/Downloads/Situational%20Leadership%20Model%20(1).pdf on May 16, 2017.

Sparrow, K. (2017). *Ignite Your Leadership Proven Tools for Leadership*. Melbourne, FL: Motivational Press.

Spears, L. C. (2002). *Focus on leadership: Servant leadership for the 21st century*. New York: Wiley.

Spears, L. C. (2010). *Servant leadership and Robert K. Greenleaf's legacy*. In D. van

Thompson, K. N. (2010). *Servant-Leadership: An Effective Model for Project Management.*

REFERENCES

Capella University Dissertation. Ann Arbor, MI: ProQuest.

Thoms, P., & Pinto J. K. (1999). Project leadership: a question of timing. *ProjectManagement Journal, 30*(1), 19-26.

Turner, J., & Muller, R. (2005). The project manager's leadership style as a success factor on projects: A literature review. *Project Management Journal, 36*(2), 49-61.

Verma, V. K. (1996). *Human Resource Skills, for the Project Manager*. Sylva, NC: PMI Publication.

Wills, K.R. (2015). *Assessing IT Projects to Ensure Successful Outcomes.* Cambridge, UK: IT Governance Publishing.

Yeager, W.P. (2017). *Testing Project Outcomes*. Amazon Digital.

APPENDIX

DALE LEADERSHIP EFFECTIVENESS MATRIX

DALE LEADERSHIP EFFECTIVENESS MATRIX

Dale Leadership Effectiveness Matrix
(1) Select which of the *10 Leadership Styles* are closely aligned with your personal or professional approach. (2) Evaluate the *7 Commitments to Highly Effective Leadership*. (3) Find the corresponding circle that indicates the degree by which the commitment can enhance your leadership style's effectiveness.

Degrees of enhancement: SMALL ○ · MODERATE ○ · LARGE ○

Copyright © 2023 by Dr. Michael Dale. All rights reserved.

10 Leadership Styles for Highly Effective Project Managers

7 Commitments to Highly Effective Leadership	Project Pro	Skills-based	Style	Situational	Path-Goal	Contingency	Emotional Intelligence	Christian	Servant	Transformational
1. Commit to Self-Awareness:										
· Spend the majority of your time improving on your strengths and what you do well.			● (L, yellow)		● (S, yellow)				● (S, yellow)	
· Don't spend significant effort addressing weaknesses especially if you can delegate something you do not do well to someone else.				● (L, yellow)				● (S, yellow)		
· Inwardly reflect on your thoughts and behaviors to gain insights into your actions and how they impact others. Make adjustments to gain positive and favorable reactions from others.	● (S, yellow)	● (S, yellow)				● (L, yellow)				
2. Commit to being Proactive:										
· Take the initiative to identify and pursue opportunities that meet your personal requirements and not just the requirements of others.	● (S, orange)	● (L, orange)	● (M, orange)		● (M, orange)	● (S, orange)		● (L, orange)	● (L, orange)	
· Break down larger goals into smaller, achievable tasks and incrementally accomplish the small goals one by one.				● (S, orange)			● (M, orange)			
· Demonstrate a willingness to go above and beyond basic expectations; however always under promise and over deliver.										● (M, orange)

141

DALE LEADERSHIP EFFECTIVENESS MATRIX

10 Leadership Styles for Highly Effective Project Managers

7 Commitments to Highly Effective Leadership	Project Pro	Skills-based	Style	Situational	Path-Goal	Contingency	Emotional Intelligence	Christian	Servant	Transformational
3. Commit to being Accountable:										
· Prioritize tasks and activities based on importance, urgency, and severity. Problems (issues) should be fixed as soon as possible; a risk should have a remediation plan to prevent future negative impacts.										●
· Set realistic, achievable deadlines and manage your time based on your capacity. This is the definition of accountability.				●	●	●		●	●	
· Avoid procrastination and stay focused on completing high-priority tasks on time while positioning lower priority items on a backlog.			●				●			
4. Commit to being Responsible:										
· The buck stops with you as a leader. Accept the fact that your head will roll if something goes wrong. Loyal team members will be cognizant of your dilemma and work very hard to be accountable.	○			○	●		○			○
· Solve problems today. A problem is an impediment that is causing a delay, overrun or rework; therefore, it must be solved expeditiously so that the team is no		●				○		●	●	
· Communicate clearly and openly with the goal of answering all answerable questions. Listen actively and attentively to affirmatively understand other's viewpoints.		●								

DALE LEADERSHIP EFFECTIVENESS MATRIX

10 Leadership Styles for Highly Effective Project Managers

7 Commitments to Highly Effective Leadership	Project Pro	Skills-based	Style	Situational	Path-Goal	Contingency	Emotional Intelligence	Christian	Servant	Transformational
5. Commit to an Agile Mindset:										
· Embrace changes based on new unplanned priorities and reprioritize appropriately.			○		○					
· Fail fast and learn from mistakes. Always seek feedback and incorporate it into the next event, task, or activity. View failure as an opportunity for growth.	●						○	○	○	
· Maintain a positive attitude. Make things easy for others, not hard. An easy-going mindset is a personal favorite of mine – the old adages that say "pain equals gain" & "adversity equals progress" are dead!		●		○	○					
6. Commit to Continuously Learning:										
· Cultivate a growth mindset and a willingness to learn as a way of life.	○									
· Remain plugged in and informed about the latest trends in your industry and domain.			●	●		●			○	●
· Look for tools, techniques and best practices that improve your way of working and the lives of others.			○	○	○		○	○		
7. Commit to Building Relationships:										
· Build a strong professional network through relationships with colleagues, friends, and acquaintances.		●	●	●						
· Foster positive relationships with colleagues, mentors, and others in your industry.						●				
· Reach out periodically to others to recognize them when they have a special day, a promotion or after a recent interaction.	●	●			●					